THESILENCEOFGOD

THE**SILENCE**OF**GOD**

Helmut Thielicke

Translated by Geoffrey W. Bromiley

Oil Lamp
BOOKS LLC

Library of Congress Control Number: 2010936788

ISBN-13: 978-0-9844917-0-4

Creative Team: Brannon Ellis and Daniel Bush

Cover design by Brannon Ellis

♾ The paper used in this book is acid free and lignin free, and meets all ANSI requirements for archival quality.

Oil Lamp Books LLC advocates the responsible use of our natural resources. The text paper in this book is Sustainable Forestry Initiative Certified.

www.olbooks.com

Contents

Introduction

ONE OF THE MOST POWERFUL VOICES from the pulpit to reach us in the years after the Second World War is that of Helmut Thielicke, who exercised a striking ministry in Germany during the war and the postwar period and who is now Rector of the University of Hamburg.

Both in style and content the sermons of Thielicke, like all good sermons, are vitally relevant to the situation in which they are preached. They are in every sense tracts for the times, carrying a message both to individuals and to nations in a tragic hour.

This does not mean, however, that they are devoid of other qualities. Thielicke has an eye for the apt quotation, the striking simile and the forceful illustration from experience. The hymns of the Church are heard again in and through his addresses, and the influence of Luther may be constantly discerned. For all their vividness, the sermons also bear marks of forceful arrangement. If they are not literary exercises or systematic treaties, they are also very far from being disconnected or spasmodic.

It should be noted, too, that the work of Thielicke is through and through theological. His theology not unnaturally takes on an existential character. Many of the great themes are those we meet with in the work of great contemporary theologians like Barth. On the other hand, Thielicke himself never confuses preaching with dogmatic theology. The theological material is assimilated and presented in terms of application to the current situation. The theology of Thielicke is a sustaining note which gives solidity to the whole.

The "existentialism" of Thielicke does not mean that his sermons are lacking in biblical content. To be sure, he is not primarily an expositor, though a thread of exposition does in fact run through some of the sermons. On the other hand, he patently takes his themes and concerns from Holy Scripture, and what he offers as his message to those who stand under postwar tragedies and tensions is supremely the biblical word, declared with almost prophetic authority and finding its focus and center in Jesus Christ.

From the standpoint of pure exegesis or dogma, deficiencies may well be found in Thielicke's presentation, and his sermons will naturally lose much of their point and thrust if we are privileged to pass out of the present storms into a calmer historical epoch. These possible weaknesses, however, give us the clue to the strength of Thielicke. He has a vivid awareness of the actual needs of actual people living in this age of supreme storm and stress. He sees how the biblical message, how Jesus Christ himself as the living message, answers powerfully and sufficiently to these needs. He appreciates that faith in him is not an easy thing, and yet that true faith carries us to victory even in doubt, anxiety, distress and the terrors of conflict and destruction. He attains almost an apocalyptic stature in his depiction of our shattered world and in his proclamation of the message of God's salvation and judgements within it.

Based as they are on the great themes of the Gospel, the sermons for Christmas, Good Friday, Easter and Pentecost in Part II of this collection, offer us a fine example of Thielicke's work, and especially of the way in which he applies the central message of the incarnation, crucifixion and resurrection to our contemporary needs. But we do less than justice to the preacher if we read his work merely with a view to critical appreciation. Here are sermons to put into the hands of contemporaries who suffer from the fears and anxieties which Thielicke so graphically describes but who do not yet perceive the true meaning and relevance of what God did for man in the giving of his only Son. Here are sermons from which to learn how the old Gospel, first given in a very different world, may come with all the living comfort and the regenerative force of truth and reality to our own age too, made relevant by the Holy Spirit on the lips of the sensitive and dedicated preacher.

G. W. Bromiley

Preface

THE FOLLOWING PAGES were composed in the extraordinary years 1942–1951. Because of the extreme relevance of the situation and the need to express it, there has been no softening or smoothing. Spiritual meditations stand side by side with words to those in supreme danger, and the excitement of the hour is everywhere manifest.

Basically, life may be reduced to a few elementary questions and certain fundamental truths. These emerge in hours of crisis when we are threatened, or seem to be threatened, by fire and water, dagger and poison, when we come to the very frontier of death, when we lose our dearest friends and when we are anxious and guilty. At such times mere reflection cannot comfort us and much that seemed to fill and even to sustain our lives is shown to be artificial. We have to leave all the carefully tended peripheral fields of life, the extras, and to retreat to the basic lines.

Our own age with its catastrophes, bombing, mass burials and evacuations is a time like this. It allows no place for comfortable thoughts or the luxury of speculation. As soldiers must be physically lean and hard in war, so our thoughts must be all muscle, skin and bone, and therefore genuine and enduring.

They will not come from the desk of the philosopher or essayist. They must be those of men who stand at graves or smoking ruins, who see houses fall and can sense there is within them a soul in need. They may have to be expressed before distracted people whose eyes still reflect the glare of the last air raid and who thus have very accurate scales by which to assess the message.

Or perhaps they are written to the exhausted or dying at the front, who have no time for silk or crystal but only for sterling metal.

Such thoughts, being designed to strengthen, are always conveyed in an actual situation, as Sartre would say. They belong to a dialogue between those affected. They are for a particular historical moment—as such thoughts will always be—and this must also be expressed. Hence there is no abstract distillation, which would be like summarizing a poem in a few sentences in the false view that this makes it unnecessary to read it and that the poet need not have woven his message into many situations, dialogues or events.

Though the sermons hardly meet the claim of the hour, though they can hardly claim to contain the hard, pure metal of truth, though the only too human sounds of "sounding brass and tinkling cymbal" are not avoided, yet their message is proclaimed in a day of extreme trial, and it is fitting that the historical situation should be reflected, not that they may have documentary value, but that it may be seen how the eternal Word comes into our human times and sustains and guides us as a reality.

The actual compilation has been done, not by the author, but by Dr. Walter Bähr, who on his own initiative took the trouble to work through the relevant material and to assemble the present chapters.

He did this, not for the past, but for the present, believing that we should not lose sight of these darkest hours in our lives but use them as a standard to discern between true light and mere will o' the wisps. Nietzsche would perhaps have said that we should preserve a record of the period as one of "monumental history"; but he, of course, would have found the monumental aspect, not in the pathos of human possibilities, but in the divine summons by which we are visited. The hour of need has typical and lasting significance because it is concentrated from the hour of the world in which we know anxiety and may thus find proof of that which claims to have overcome the world.

Perhaps the call will still go out to those—ourselves included—who even now face anxiety and guilt, suffering and death.

It may be that the difference in situations gives rise to great difference in language, so that the identity of the author is almost lost. The basic idea of the book carries with it the risk of this type of expression. It would naturally be impermissible in a book of essays. But it is perhaps a reflection of the troubled life to which the message is addressed. Indeed, it perhaps bears testimony to the other life which the message itself proclaims. This is at least the hope of the author.

Helmut Thielicke

PART ONE

Anxiety and Its Cure

1

I am Not Alone with My Anxiety

SOME TIME AGO, according to a technique similar to that of the Gallup polls, a number of questions were put to mainly young people, for the most part students. One of them was as follows: "What is your basic reaction to life?" Sixty percent answered with alarming definiteness: "Anxiety." How is it that so many who make no impression of being depressed or worried can give such a strange reply?

When we think in terms of anxiety, we are usually inclined to imagine that it arises from a mortal threat, that it is fear of death. But if we use this concept to check the correctness of the poll in question, we shall not get very far. It can hardly be said of our generation that it is particularly afraid of death. I hardly need to adduce in proof examples from the war, and especially from wartime bombing. It has often been observed with surprise that one does not have to be religious not to be afraid of death. The apathetic, the atheists and nihilists, can all show a definite nonchalance in face of mortal peril, and even an idealistic readiness for death. Thus Communist soldiers were found to be more afraid of physical pain than of actual death, and this points to a most astonishing conquest of the fear of death in the very circles which seem to be completely without the consolation and support of religion.

But perhaps I am mistaken in speaking of the conquest of the fear of death. For the obvious point is that there was no such fear to conquer. The fear of death had no genuine opponent to overcome. The terrors of the hereafter are banished from the nihilist world, so that death is no longer an overwhelming catastrophe. There is no spirit to yield up nor soul to lose.

At all events, one cannot say that the fear of death is particularly common in our day. Certainly the answer that anxiety is the basic reaction does not refer to fear of death. To what, then, does it refer?

We may safely assume that it refers to the fear of life rather than of death. If the middle–aged monk Martin Luther was filled with anxious guilt in face of the divine Judge, and had to ask how he could find a gracious God, so modern man is afflicted by fear of destiny, by anxiety at the dreadful possibilities of life. Where once stood the divine Judge is now a vacuum, an empty spot. Perhaps it is just this blank which evokes in us the dreadful *horror vacui*, the fear of emptiness. Perhaps instead of asking with Luther how to find the gracious God we are really asking where God is. Where is he in face of the mass slaughter of war, or the frightening development of technics which seems to press us inexorably towards destruction and final catastrophe?

In the place of guilt and judgment we may now speak of anxiety and destiny. Anxiety is the secret wound of modern man.

To understand it, we should consider its linguistic root. It derives from the Latin *angustiae*, which signifies constriction of breathing, *angina pectoris* being a maximal form. It is typical that anxiety refers to a state in which the question what is feared is either secondary or is not even asked. The indefiniteness of the threat is of the very essence of anxiety.

Fear always refers to something definite. I am afraid of getting wet because of certain meteorological factors. Or I am afraid of a political complication in view of certain observations and developments.

What causes anxiety, however, is the indefinite. In this respect anxiety is like boredom. I am simply anxious, as I am bored. There is no definite cause.

Yet we have not reached the heart of the matter if we understand anxiety only in terms of individual constriction. It is not merely my personal breathing which is constricted by this mysterious unknown. It is the supra–personal breathing of the world. Perhaps the Midgard serpent of German mythology is illuminating in this respect. Beyond the horizon the great serpent encircles the world, enclosing us in its grasp. The whole world is encircled by this dreadful monster. Its shadow and terror are on all things, even on our joys and festivities in the world which is thus so terribly encircled. This will help us to understand the full terror of anxiety. When I am just afraid, when I fear something definite, I can always hope. Thus, if I am afraid I have cancer, it may be I have only a non–malignant growth, or there is always the chance of an unexpected cure. Again, if I am afraid that a missing son is dead, he may well be alive, possibly in a concentration camp from which he will return. But under the constriction of the Midgard serpent the case is very different. For now the whole world, with all its hopes and fears, is called in question; even the gods to whom we pray, and therefore the powers of hope, lie under the shadow of the twilight of the gods. In times of disaster the serpent is, so to speak, tightening its coils.

What is the source of this anxiety for modern man? I am not going to give a theoretical answer. I will simply quote a well–known vision which discloses the source of our anxiety in a way which is terrifying and yet comforting. I refer to Christ's address from the world temple to say that there is no God, by Jean Paul. Jean Paul is here imagining that there is no God. Christ himself acknowledges in a shattering sermon that he was mistaken in his belief in God and that we are all orphans.

The author sees himself set above a burial ground. A corpse on the bier in the church raises its hands and folds them in prayer, but the arms become elongated and drop off, the folded hands with them. On the roof of the church stands the clock face of eternity, but there are no numbers and it is its own indicator. A black finger points to it, and the dead want to see the time on it.

A lofty and noble figure now comes down with infinite sorrow from above to the altar, and all the dead cry "Christ, is there no God?"

He answers: "There is none."

Christ continues: "I have been through the worlds, ascended to the suns and flown along the milky ways trough the wastes of heaven, but there is no God. I have descended as far as existence casts its shadow and looked into the abyss and cried: 'Father, where art Thou?' But I have heard only the eternal tempest which none controls, and with no sun to fashion it the glistening rainbow from the west stood over the abyss and dripped down. And when I searched the immeasurable world for the divine eye it fixed me with an empty and unfathomable socket, and eternity lay on chaos and gnawed it away and repeated itself. Lament and cry through the shadows, for he is not." The vision continues.

Then in a way to rend the heart dead infants, raised from the graveyard, come into the temple, and fling themselves before the lofty figure on the alter and say: "Jesus, have we no Father?" And he answers with streaming tears: "We are all orphans, I and you, we have no Father.... O blank, dumb nothingness! O cold eternal necessity! O mad caprice! Do you know this? When will you destroy the building and Me?... How each is alone in the vast tomb of the whole! I am alone—O Father! O Father! Where is thine infinite bosom on which to rest? Oh, if each I is his own father and creator, why not his own destroying angel?..."

Here are all the elements of anxiety as we have come to see it. It is anxiety in face of the endless void, silent nothingness, the dreadful lawlessness of a fatherless world. The awful thing in this situation is thus the fact that men are without hope. There are no ultimate sanctions. This is why Dostoevsky says that everything is permitted. This is why man is so cruel to man. There results the situation depicted by Sartre in his play *No Exit*. Hell consists in the facts that men vaunt themselves against one another and torment one another and fight for power and security. And all this leads to nothing, because the throbbing heart has been taken from the world and it has no more goal or basis.

It would be surprising if man did nothing to try to rid himself of his anxiety. How he does so is impressively stated in Ernst Jünger's essay *Man in the Moon*: "In respect of meaning, that is, recognizable order in history, my existence is hopeless, and therefore harassing, like nothing else on earth. I, as man on the moon, can nowhere find sense, being truly in an icy lunar world with its craters. Since I have given up seeking the point of my life, I am completely tormented." The attempt to escape anxiety does not now take the Faustian form of trying to find meaning, but of living only for the day and therefore of vegetating.

Man does not free himself from anxiety or meaninglessness by continually putting the question of meaning and succor, but by not putting it, by ceasing to be man, by making himself anonymous, by smothering himself in the mass, or by becoming the executive organ of processes and functions whose purpose and goal no longer concern him. Here rest is found. It is the deceptive peace of a technical nirvana, of self–immolation. It is a flight to the foreground, to the surface. We see this everywhere in modern life. There are few aspects of modern life which do not bear this mark of anxiety and flight therefrom on their forehead.

This brings us to the question whether there can be any genuine conquest of anxiety instead of this deceptive evasion.

The Christian cannot speak of this conquest without thinking of the One who said: "In the world you will have tribulation. But take heart; I have overcome the world." But this statement obviously needs to be interpreted if we are to avoid empty consolation.

It first tells us that the powers of guilt, suffering and death have been overcome by this One. Perhaps it is a fatal one–sidedness of Christian churches that they see Christ only in the context of victory over guilt, of forgiveness and justification. Rightly or wrongly, many men think that this reveals a failure to understand their deepest problems. The New Testament, however, speaks of suffering and death as well as sin. And these are the powers of anxiety because they represent the threat of the meaningless. Suffering always raises the question whether joy and pain are not arbitrarily allotted, whether life is not an uncharted journey into the void. We have only to think of the despair of Job. Death, too, casts the shadow of meaninglessness. Therefore let us eat, drink and be merry; for tomorrow we die. Eating and drinking here signify the silencing of anxiety.

The surprising thing in the biblical message is that it finds in love the opposite of fear and anxiety. There is no terror—one might equally well say anxiety—in love, we are told in 1 John. The surprising thing is that anxiety is not opposed by fortitude, courage or heroism, as one might expect. These are simply anxiety suppressed, not conquered. The positive force which defeats anxiety is love. What this means can be understood only when we have tackled anxiety in what we have tried to see as its final root. That is to say, anxiety is a broken bond and love is the bond restored. Once we know in Christ that the world has a fatherly basis and that we are loved, we lose our anxiety. This is not because the powers referred to have gone. On Dürer's picture of the Horseman, Death and the Devil, they lurk on the way. But they have lost their strength. To use a simple comparison—and simplicity is needed in ultimate questions—I need have no fear even in the darkest forest when I hold my father's hand and I am sure of it.

Christ himself faces the constricting riddles of life. According to the oldest record, his final word on the cross is the anxious cry: "My God, my God, why have you forsaken me?" It is characteristic, however, that he does not address this cry of despair into the night of Golgotha. He calls to his Father: "My God, my God." He holds the Father's hand firm in his own. He brings the anxiety to his Father. He has brought it once and for all. If I am anxious, and I know Christ, I may rest assured that I am not alone with my anxiety; He has suffered it for me. The believer can also know that Christ is the goal of history. The primitive community knows that this One has not gone forever, but will come again. It thus has a new relationship to the future. This is no longer a mist–covered landscape into which I peer anxiously because of the sinister events which will there befall me. Everything is now different. We do not know what will come. But we know who will come. And if the last hour belongs to us, we do not need to fear the next minute.

2

The Silence of God[*]

And Jesus went away from there and withdrew to the district of Tyre and Sidon. And behold, a Canaanite woman from that region came out and was crying, "Have mercy on me, O Lord, Son of David; my daughter is severely oppressed by a demon." But he did not answer her a word. And his disciples came and begged him, saying, "Send her away, for she is crying out after us." He answered, "I was sent only to the lost sheep of the house of Israel." But she came and knelt before him, saying, "Lord, help me." And he answered, "It is not right to take the children's bread and throw it to the dogs." She said, "Yes, Lord, yet even the dogs eat the crumbs that fall from their masters' table." Then Jesus answered her, "O woman, great is your faith! Be it done for you as you desire." And her daughter was healed instantly.

Matthew 15:21–28

THIS WOMAN IS ONE of the secondary and marginal figures in the world of the New Testament. She does not stand in

---

[*] Preached in 1943 during the battle of Stalingrad.

the spotlight like the main characters in the history of Jesus of Nazareth. She is not a disciple or a high priest or a prophet or a Pilate. All these help to push the wheel of history. They all know something about Jesus as followers or opponents in the great drama then being enacted on the world stage. This woman neither advances the history nor has any essential knowledge. She can make no profession of faith. She is quite unaffected by the question whether Jesus will conquer the world or whether he must suffer. She certainly has no inkling of the Christ problem. She is a poor unknown beyond the boarder of Tyre and Sidon. She is a secondary figure, such as those we can see in the obscure light on the margin of the paintings of Rembrandt. Yet on this figure who had no knowledge and contributed nothing to history there suddenly falls the light of the eyes of Jesus. He speaks to her the surprising word: "Great is your faith!" He has never said this to any of his disciples who left all for his sake. To only one other has he said it, and that was given to an unnamed secondary figure, the centurion of Capernaum.

What has she done that Jesus should thus extol her faith? She has simply met him and stretched out her hand to him.

There are some of us who cannot make anything of one or another dogma or who have doubts that they cannot resolve. They should prick up their ears and hear about this great faith. For it does not consist in regarding something as true, or in a capacity for dogmatic understanding, but in a struggle, in a dialogue with God.

We can easily see what course this dialogue takes. There is outcry and gesticulation. The need is laid before God. Then there is silence. There are dangerous pauses. There are moments when understanding breaks off, when crises arise, when it seems any moment as though one or the other will get up and go. And then finally accord is reached, and Jesus stands up, stretches forth his hand for time and eternity and says: "Well done, you faithful child...." Silence, rejection, pauses, acceptance—all have their place in this dialogue. Those who want to speak with Jesus should pay attention, for we are about to consider one of the most profound and indeed unfathomable stories in the New Testament.

How is it that the woman comes to Jesus? We are simply told: "And behold, a Canaanite woman from that region came out." Yet these colorless words are not without significance. For to come she has to overcome the prejudices of her people against the figure of the Nazarene. She has even to cross the frontier of another land. She has to enter a country which in nationality and outlook is divided by an abyss from all that is accepted around her. Finally, her coming involves risk. She knows of him only by hearsay. Perhaps the reports are deceptive. She has to accept the possibility not merely that her action will be disappointingly futile but that it will leave her open to censure.

But all faith begins this way. We have to cross the frontier of the centuries to approach the Nazarene. We have to cross the frontier of a foreign land which is distant and strange. We have always to cross the frontier of the great events around us and to enter the stillness which surrounds Jesus and which moves and shakes the world more than all the Vulcan strokes of historical catastrophes and revelations which in these days shatter the earth. This, then, is how she comes to Jesus.

But quick though she is, she is no match for Jesus of Nazareth. There are tests and pauses and silences. Luther says that the woman had first to be buffeted before help was given to her.

Jesus is first silent in face of her request: "*He did not answer her a word.*" The silence of God is the greatest test of our faith. We all know this. It is natural that we should think of the title of Dwinger's book, *And God Is Silent*, which he accusingly adopts as a motto for the terrible events in Russia. But why refer to books! Can we not all sing about this today? Can we not shriek it out? Is not God silent about Stalingrad? What do we hear above and under its ruins? Do we not hear the roar of artillery, the tumult of the world and the cries of the dying? But where is the voice of God? When we think of God, is it not suddenly so quiet, so terribly quiet, in the witches' kitchen of this hell, that one can hear a pin drop even though grenades are bursting around us? There is neither voice nor answer. And even if I think I hear God—hear him in judgement as the One by whom the proud waves are stayed (Job 38:11)—he is silent again the next moment when I have to ask: Why this man, my brother or my husband?

Just like ourselves, John the Baptist was tortured by questions in prison; and there is great comfort in the fact that it is not only we men of the twentieth century who put such God–forsaken questions and suffer under the silence of God. The Baptist, too, put the anxious question: What sense is there, and does it not drive us mad, that the so–called Messiah moves about with his disciples in the sunshine while his herald is so completely incarcerated behind impregnable walls and stands under threat of death? In despairing complaint he rises against this destiny of the silence of Jesus. "How long do you keep us in suspense? Tell us freely whether you are Christ." Call down from heaven that you are. Do you not see how dreadful are the effects of your silence? Do you not see how much more merciful it would be if this voice were to ring out so that all would have to hear it, and would not therefore be put on the rack and plunged into the torment of uncertainty? Why do you allow this vacillation between faith and doubt? Why do you not make things clear, God?

Men would not keep silence for so long about what is happening. They could not see so much blood shed or hear the cry of sufferers so long. Does this mean that they are more merciful? Not at all! The disciples are men who cannot bear the silence of Jesus or see the distress of the woman. But not by a long way does this mean that they are more merciful. The woman senses this; otherwise she would have turned to the weary and therefore more helpful disciples. She realizes, however, that they are not merciful in yielding to her cry for help. They have poor nerves. This makes some people seem to be sympathetic and neighborly. But they are not. The invalid and the wayside beggar do not really believe in the mercy of men. Otherwise they would not utter so frequently their moving complaints.

The woman turns rather to the silent Jesus than to men. Obviously the silence of God is to be measured by other standards than that of men. The Canaanite woman gropes behind the silence. Even though she has to tarry the night long and till morning, her heart will not despair of God's power nor be afraid. So it often is when God does not answer our prayers. Behind the silence are his higher thoughts. He is fitting stone to stone in his plan for the world and our lives, even though we can see only a confused and meaningless jumble of stones heaped together under a silent heaven. How many meaningless blows of fate there seem to be!—life, suffering, injustice, death, massacres, destruction; and all under a silent heaven which apparently has nothing to say. The cross was God's greatest silence. Then the power of darkness was allowed to make its final bid against the Son of God. Then the demons were unleashed and the most dreadful passions since the fall of Adam were given free rein. And God had nothing to say. There was simply the cry of the Dying asking of the silence why God has forsaken him. God was still silent even when dumb nature began to speak in an eloquent gesture and the sun withdrew its light. The stars cried out, and God was silent.

But now hear the great mystery of this silence. The very hour when God answered not a word or syllable was the hour of the great turning point when the veil of the temple was rent and God's heart was laid bare with all its wounds. Even when he was silent, God suffered with us. In his silence he experienced the fellowship of death and the depths with us. Even when we thought he did not care, or was dead, he knew all about us and behind the dark wings he did his work of love. We live in the power of this Golgotha night of silence. Where should we be without the cross? Where should we be without the knowledge that God sends his Son to us in the silent depths and valleys, that he is our Fellow in death; that he has indeed his high thoughts, that they come with power at Easter in glorious fulfillments surpassing all our expectations?

Truly the silence of God is different from that of men. When Jesus lay silent and asleep in the ship, he was more kind and his arm was more near to help and more certain than the anxious cry of the doubting disciples suggests. The silence of God and of Jesus is not of indifference. It is the silence of higher thoughts. It does not imply a silent destiny. The woman sees this. Hence she persists in spite of the silence and does not let her hands fall.

There follows the second rebuff and therewith the second test of faith. The silence is suddenly broken. Low speech is heard, from which two sentences stand out, first: "I was sent only to the lost sheep of the house of Israel;" and second: "It is

not right to take the children's bread and throw it to the dogs."
This obviously means that you are not one of the children who
are my concern.

Between these gloomy statements there is only the cry: "Lord,
help me!"; and this cry, which ascends like a rocket, is encircled
and apparently quenched by the power of the divine silence.

What is Jesus trying to convey? Simply that it is an integral
part of God's plan of salvation to begin his work in Israel. It is
at this lowest point of the great burden of humanity that he will
first bring relief. Only when this has been done will he extend
his work. So far, however, this first task has not been completed.
The turn of the Gentiles has not yet come. Jesus is not yet avail-
able to this woman. In other words, the woman has to see that,
while God is good, he is not good for me. Jesus Christ is the
Savior, but he is not my Savior. There is a communion of saints,
but I do not belong to it.

Have we not all had similar experiences? Many can confess today how kind is this Jesus of Nazareth. We should like to
dwell in his peace. In bitter hours many good words concerning him have soothed and restored us like a mother's hand. And
when many of us hear this word we will perhaps go away like
Faust on Easter night, when at a very dangerous and desperate
moment in his life, the poisoned cup already at his lips, he suddenly heard the Easter bells which evoked magical recollection
of his home and childhood. For many the words of Jesus will
perhaps be a similar magic, greeting us from afar.

But then comes the bitter realization: "I do not belong to
him." Why not? There are so many puzzling features about this
figure. There is the cross, the resurrection. There are the dogmas. I should like to dwell in his place, but there are so many
things in the Church and Christianity that I can make nothing

of. I should like to receive his good words like balsam, but I cannot swallow these other things. And finally—this is the ultimate obstacle—I find it impossible to be a Christian when there are so many objections, when God so often seems to be so terribly unjust and human arrogance triumphs, when faith in love and righteousness is left in the lurch and when the loving Father above the pavilion of the stars is just a childish dream. How can I be a Christian? I can perhaps agree that those to whom faith is given, who can accept all this, are fortunate. But faith is not given to me. I do not belong.

How many speak like this and therefore understand the woman of Canaan: I do not belong; I cannot belong. And many think they know just why. It is all a matter, they say, of whether one can or not. Either one has this faith or not. Either one enjoys this gift or it is denied. I just cannot believe. I do not have the gift. I am left out. How fortunate are those who have it. I think of the many streets where I have walked with good friends, and many evenings in the barracks. Our conversations about the figure of Jesus always closed with the words: I cannot; I do not belong. I think of them now, those friends, who during these conversations about Jesus of Nazareth looked from afar at a land for which they longed but from which they thought they were excluded. "You must understand," said one, "that it is not given to me; I do not have the knack. I should like to, and I will give you my hand when you go to the cross. It is too bad. We share everything else and agree at all other points."

I see them now, those good friends. And perhaps there are many like them here today—those who say: "It is not given to me, I do not belong."

Well, consider the readiness of this woman who does not merely think but is actually told authoritatively: "You do not belong." What does she do and what is her great faith in this situation? Her faith is not the possession of a special talent for swallowing difficult dogmas and necessary articles of faith, of which we hear nothing. Nor is it the enjoyment of a particular religious or metaphysical endowment, nor the lack of sufficient critical or intellectual ability to appreciate the objections.

Her faith is simply her trust that he can help me, so that she can only call upon him and hunger and thirst after this Savior. It is already faith, my friends, to see in oneself something of the hunger and thirst after this high and helping figure, and to surrender to it and come to Jesus. It is the hungry and thirsty and sorrowful who are called blessed by this Jesus, and does he not pronounce his "Well done" to those who cannot boast of the sufficiency or correctness of their dogmatic belief:

> *Nothing of my own I bring,*
> *You, O Lord, are everything.*

Those who have a hungry heart and broken spirit are the favorites of God.

There are two ways of dealing with this hunger and thirst, with this longing which we all know. One way is to suppress it instead of giving it free rein, smothering it under the little business of the day with its cares and pleasures.

The other is to take the risk of simply coming to Jesus like this woman. And truly we should take this risk, for it is true, as Augustine has said, that we could not seek God if he had not already found us. If this woman is not reluctant it is because the Lord is not reluctant—in spite of his silence.

The conversation proceeds. Indeed, it reaches its climax. We hold our breath. How will the woman react to the statement of Jesus that there is a wall of partition between them? Will she emphasize her need? Will she appeal to her great faith? Will she act like the cripple by the wayside? Will she speculate on the pity of God? Will she give way to what Walter Flex has called the coward's prayer of panic? Will she begin to whine? No. There takes place something very strange and unexpected. She says: "Truth, Lord." This means that I accept the justice of your silence, of your ignoring me. It is by no means self–evident that you should help me. You are right to pass on, Jesus of Naza-reth. I have no claim on you.

We do well to grasp the tremendous implication of this thought. For it is to the effect that my acceptance by God cannot be taken for granted. That Jesus died on the cross for me cannot be taken for granted. We European Christians have gradually become accustomed to the dangerous and unhealthy idea that the grace of God is thrown at us. Voltaire cynically said of the forgiveness of God: "*C'est son métier* — it is his job." But this is not so. Things are quite different from the popular assumption. The kingdom of God is not thrust on us. The grace of God can also be silent. We certainly cannot claim it. It may be, and if so I cannot blame God, that in my last hour I will sink into darkness and the one figure who might be with me through the gloomy portal will be missing. It is in no sense the duty or obligation of Jesus to bear my sin and to take me through the black gate of death. If he does this, it cannot be taken for granted. And I make bold to say that even the most orthodox churchman will not enter the kingdom of heaven unless he is continually sur-prised that mercy has been shown him. We cannot say that we do not merit wrath or that grace must be ours. There is rising up among us a host of young Christians who are tired of the new paganism. They can describe this astonishment far more clear-ly and realistically than those who have inherited the secure tradition of the fathers. I refer to the astonishment that there is more than a great transcendant God beyond the stars, that there is a condescension and forgiveness and God's sorrow for his children. Perhaps God has first to be jerked away from us complacent Western Christians, like a rug from under our feet, if we are to be reawakened to this surprise.

All this is implied in the "Truth, Lord." The tormented woman allows that grace may justly pass her by. Hence she has no thought of cursing Jesus.

We are now nearing the end of the dramatic dialogue. The woman continues: "Yet even the dogs eat the crumbs that fall from their master's table." Yet—is there not here a contradiction after her previous unconditional acceptance? Is she not withdrawing and becoming illogical?

This lack of logic—if we may call it such—is the whole secret of prayer. We see it is in the Lord's Prayer. For we say "Your will be done," which is the same as "Truth, Lord," but we still ask for our daily bread and many other things. How are we to explain this contradiction? As I say, this is the deepest mystery of prayer.

For we know to whom we are saying "Your will be done" when we ask God to fulfill his will and thus to shape our own. The petition does not mean that I must be resigned. That is no use. No, the "Truth, Lord" is spoken with a joyous undertone, for the woman knows with whom she is dealing. And when she says "Truth" the word contains her full confidence that he will put things right. For it is assent to the love of Jesus, even though to his hidden love which waits behind the silence and in spite of his refusal, ready to break out in glory and favor and to call this woman of faith blessed. Hence this woman will not draw back when the night of the cross comes and all others flee. She will not go astray when persecutions arise, when terror reigns, when God is silent and when the love of the faithful grows cold. For she will then know that God has higher thoughts in relation to the world and that the ways of peace are trodden. It is because she has the courage to say "'Truth, Lord" that she can cheerfully go on to ask: "Yet...." This "Yet" implies that I have not deserved to belong to you, that I have no claim on you, that you pass by, Savior of Nazareth.

But can you? Can you pass by someone who renounces all his merits—his achievements, his moral rectitude, even his great faith? Can you pass by someone who sets all these aside and expects everything only of your love and generous hands? Can you do this, Savior of Nazareth?

Jesus cannot. As Luther says, "This woman takes Jesus in his own words," and especially in the saying that he loves the hungry and thirsty and the spiritually poor, and that he will not despise a contrite heart. She has done what none other could do, namely, entangle the Savior in his talk. She has "flung the sack of his promises at his feet," and he cannot step over it.

It is not her great faith that has triumphed. She has triumphed because she has taken the Savior at his word. She has caused the heart of God to prevail against the silence of God. This is why she has great faith. And this is why she will not be the least in the kingdom of heaven.

We should apply this profound story to our own lives that it may also be true of us.

We should wrestle with this Lord, as the woman of Canaan did, even when he seems to be silent. We should not let him go until he blesses us. We should show him our empty, longing hands. And he, who gives his children bread and not stones, who showed grace to a poor woman even though she was no churchwoman and enjoyed no high esteem, will also extend his grace to those who dare not believe that they are called and elect, but who yet pray every hour:

"Truth, Lord" and "Have mercy upon us."

3

The Question of Christ

"The baptism of John, from where did it come? From heaven or from man?" And they discussed it among themselves, saying, "If we say, 'From heaven,' he will say to us, 'Why then did you not believe him?' But if we say, 'From man,' we are afraid of the crowd, for they all hold that John was a prophet." So they answered Jesus, "We do not know." And he said to them, "Neither will I tell you by what authority I do these things."

Matthew 21:25–27

THE SO-CALLED "LOVING SAVIOR," whom we always like to picture as the One who blessed the children, who with infinite patience seeks the lost, and who pardons his sadistic executioners, the so-called loving Savior here ends a discussion on agitated and important questions of faith by closing the door with a loud bang and leaving his hearers. Is this how a pastoral conversation should end?

There is an almost unbearable tension in this story. It begins with the question: "By what authority are you doing these things, and who gave you this authority?" (v. 24). This question obviously seems to derive from an honest concern. And yet the conversation closes with the crisp statement of Jesus: "Neither will I tell you by what authority I do these things" (v. 27).

Are we not shocked and rebuffed by this refusal? What are we to say about it? Above all, what did these people do that Jesus dealt so hardly with them? For obviously they must have done something serious.

Many of us complain that God is so dreadfully quiet, and that particularly when dealing with Christ we seem to stand before a closed door. We may even conclude that there is nothing in the whole story; otherwise there would be more to catch our attention. In face of this situation we must ask whether this deathly silence, this constricting stillness surrounding God, is not due to the fact that he wills to be silent because we are not yet in a position in which he can speak to us.

However that may be, we see at once that this is a question affecting our own lives and that we are implicated in this story in a very direct and inescapable way.

As we have said, the story begins with the coming to Jesus of some ecclesiastical dignitaries who ask him by what authority he performs his acts, and who has given him this authority. Who are you? How did this question arise?

By his words and acts and manner Jesus had made a powerful impression on these men. He spoke very differently from other preachers. It was said of him that he spoke with authority and not as the scribes and Pharisees. What was the difference? Did he speak more passionately, or forcefully, or persuasively? Did he know more of the things of God? We do not know. All these things are possible. But they are not the decisive things.

The decisive thing is this. The preachers (and therefore the scribes and Pharisees) very earnestly declared the will of God in his Law, speaking of the fatherly love with which he seeks us, of his forgiveness and of his covenant with men. Jesus handled the same themes, but in a surprisingly different way. For he did not speak about these things. As he spoke, he entered into the things of God in an active and creative way which changes the whole situation. Thus, when he met a guilty man, he did not preach a sermon or deliver a lecture on the theme that God is a Judge before whom he must perish, but that God is also merciful and will perhaps justify him in grace if he will take up a right attitude to him. No, he tells such a man directly and authoritatively: "Your sins are forgiven." And as he says this the man knows that his chains fall off, that he can stand up and go away a new creature. When Jesus speaks we have more than a word; we have an enactment, a creative deed which makes things new. No man can do this. We can see by this what "authority" means in the language of the New Testament.

We have also to consider the way in which he deals with sorrow in the world, with anxiety, sickness and death. Preachers can say that the day of God is coming when all tears shall be wiped away and there shall be no more sorrow or crying. But when Jesus arrives things are different. The lame literally rise up already and begin to walk; the eyes of the blind are opened; the poor are made merry and the oppressed begin to praise. When Jesus arrives the atmosphere is full of intimations of what God will one day do fully and unmistakably. The brightening of the day of God may be seen already on the horizon.

When people see all these things, they are forced to ask him who he really is and from what source he has this power. In spite of all skepticism, antipathy, or social or philosophical objections, in face of this sensation from Nazareth, they have to say that he is absolutely different from ourselves.

Hence they put the question of his authority. Its meaning is simply this: Jesus of Nazareth, what is really behind you? Are you really different from us?

Undoubtedly there is something different. You have something about you. You have a mysterious power over men and things, and no one can perform the same signs as you.

Thus men press him throughout the centuries, trying to unlock his secret.

You have kindled a fire on earth, Nazarene. It sweeps around the globe, jumps across the seas and penetrates the most distant continents. Even centuries later it can still do this.

You have power, Jesus of Nazareth. There is no doubt about this, for no man has exerted so much influence. Millions have been imprisoned, thrown to the lions and executed for you, and have praised you with their dying breath.

There is no doubt that you have power, Jesus of Nazareth— power such as no mortal man possessed. Caesars and dictators have established kingdoms to last forever. They have strengthened their frontiers, raised mighty armies and had themselves extolled as saviors. But all their glory has vanished with the wind. New cultures and kingdoms have arisen, and they, too, have had the mark of their destruction upon them. Their brilliant rise has been inexorably followed by their decline. This is human destiny, and always will be.

But you have remained, Jesus of Nazareth. Yet you had no kingdom of military power. You did not summon the twelve legions of angels to establish your earthly rule. You had few disciples who at the critical hour in your life failed to understand you and fled.

You died on a gallows in a poor and insignificant country, and world history strode over you. But no—you strode over world history. We still hear your step. The dying on battlefields look up when you come in their last hour. The faces of the guilty brighten when you take off their chains. The anxious and care–worn find rest when they hear your voice: "Fear not." In all the poor and despised you traverse the world afresh. Your eternal journeying is in the guise of the poorest.

Yes, you have remained, puzzling Nazarene. You often seem to have been buried. For whole epochs you have been silenced. But you have always come forth from the sealed tomb and caused men to realize that you are the Savior and the secret Ruler of the world.

Thus men in all ages speak with Jesus, and they finally ask him: Do you not see how we are tormented by the question who you are and by what authority you do these things?

Who are you, Jesus of Nazareth?

Are you a personality of tremendous evocative power to be able to do all this? Are you a genius at handling men that you can bind them to you to live and die for you? Are you a clever psychologist, a skilled manipulator of souls, that you exploit the religious needs of men and make yourself indispensable to the generations?

Or—are you the Son of God? Are you the Wholly Other? Are you alone from above, where we are all from below? Does God's fatherly heart beat in you when you stoop to the sick and poor? Does God's hand act in yours when you lay it in healing on wounded consciences and diseased bodies?

Please tell us, who are you? What is the source of your power? Is it from God or from men?

And now I ask all you who are listening and who read this:

Do we not all have to put the same question? For which of us has not Jesus of Nazareth been a problem?

We can put the question as follows. Is Jesus a point in the history of religion? Is he a station in the course of its complicated development? May we not rightly suppose that this point will be finally submerged and surpassed by another, that a new religion will come more suited to the men of our technical age, more modern, more adapted to include the various viewpoints that we should like to see included? Do we not live today in an interval between Christianity and a coming religion, between "the end and the beginning," as Martin Hieronimi once put it?

Or—is Jesus the one who will someday come from the other direction to meet history when it reaches its end? Is he the only one to come to the great host of humanity from the other side? Is he the Son of Man; the King with the sickle and the crown, who on his day will come on the clouds of heaven and will be proclaimed the King of the coming kingdom? If so—we cannot look for another.

Everything depends on the answer to this question. For example, it decides the question what the Christian Church is, whether a religious union or an institution against which the gates of hell shall not prevail. It also decides the question what the Bible is, whether a literary product of antiquarian value or the book of life with all the consolations of this world and the next.

We can thus imagine how tense were the expressions of those who put the question. Their whole lives rested on this little question. If Jesus answered: "I have my authority from God, I am the meaning of history and on the last day I will come to judge the quick and the dead, as is my due"—they could not go on living as before. For their whole endeavor would be to stand clear with this Christ. Both they and I would have to consider the problem of guilt in our lives very differently. We should have to settle this decisive question. We should have to have a very different attitude to our fellow men; for this Jesus has made them our brothers and committed them to our love. We should have to do our work under his eyes, go to battle under his protection, take his hand in our loneliness and find comfort in him in our last hour.

In this one question of the Christ all our problems are grounded. This is why such electric tension rests on the story.

How great this tension can be I know from my own pastoral experience with a young believing soldier waiting for death in a hospital. The Roman Catholic priest had been before me, and the soldier had confessed and signified his resolve to become a Roman Catholic. "There must be something about this Christ," he said; he had seen it in his Christian comrades. But a few hours later the whole problem arose afresh. The question of the Christ, so long evaded, would not let him go, and with his last strength he hurled his hot water bottle at the crucifix on the wall of his sickroom.

Thus the question can even become a physical burden, especially when, as in this case, it has been constantly postponed and arises only in the last hour when there can be no more evasion.

What will Jesus do when men, when you and I, stand before him with questioning eyes? Does he not have to say Yes or No, simply for our peace of soul?

Instead he answers: "I also will ask you one question" (v. 24). He puts a counter–question.

Strictly, this is always the practice of Jesus in his pastoral conversations. He is not prepared simply to answer our problems, for example, what is the meaning of our life, whether God or fate is master, or what will happen after death. He refuses to hand us answers to these questions on a platter.

On this occasion he unexpectedly asks: "The baptism of John, from where did it come? From heaven or from man?" (v. 25).

Why does he ask this apparently irrelevant question which not only jars but also seems to miss the situation of the questioners? The only point of the question is to determine whether the question of the Christ is really of final seriousness for these people. Their seriousness can be judged by their readiness to commit themselves, to adopt a responsible position. On the basis of the counter–question of Jesus they must be ready to commit themselves before God. If they admit that John as the preacher of repentance acted and preached on divine authority, then they accept the fact that they are not right with God, for this is what John the Baptist maintained. They confess: "We who are so respected by men are poor, unhappy creatures; we must repent if God is to be able to use us. We must become new." This is what they must do without any Ifs or Buts. It is to this that they must commit themselves.

Or they must be ready to commit themselves before men and argue that John was a mistaken fanatic and pessimist. But this is dangerous, for the view is so unpopular that it involves the risk of broken heads. They might easily say that John was a fanatic. Jesus would not take it amiss. But if they do say it, they must accept the consequences. Thus Jesus can detect how serious they are. Everything depends on how serious they are, irrespective of the answer.

There is a type of religious questioner, as we see from the case of Nicodemus, who is undoubtedly not serious, who desires only to initiate great discussions of philosophical and religious themes, who revels in the obscurity of these difficult problems, who finds in them an occasion for his own academic display. He has perhaps had philosophical training, and the perspicacity of his arguments and counter–arguments is evident. All this is possible. Yet in no circumstances will the disputant commit himself. He will not decide. He is not willing to be jolted by Jesus from his course. What he says will be on the non–binding level of the intellect. It must never take on the character of ultimate decision.

We can only note that Jesus never answers this kind of person. He instructs only those who are ready to have ultimate dealings with God. He withholds himself from mere onlookers or spectators.

There are some things in life which can be known only when we are in earnest and engage in them. War is an example. Possibly the news review in the motion–picture theater might give us a more realistic portrayal of the horrors of war and the terror of bombing. Yet those who have seen these pictures cannot really say that they know what war is. Such knowledge is not to be gained in the comfortable seat of a theater. To know what war is one has to be plunged into the venture of life, into mortal anguish, into anxiety for loved ones, into deadly sorrow. The spectator in the stands may participate inwardly; but as a mere spectator of this bloody and chaotic drama he cannot really know what war is.

We can now see what Jesus is really asking in his counter–question.

Are you prepared ultimately, that is, if you see that I am the Son of God, to change and renew your whole life? Are you prepared seriously and publicly to make your confession before men even though it is unpopular, like the suggestion that the baptism of John is only human? If so, you will know who I am—but only so! Mere curiosity about Jesus of Nazareth, or pretense of seeking God, is not enough.

Only those who have a right attitude, namely, the attitude of obedience to Christ, can see him in true perspective. To do this we have to have the experience of Peter at Caesarea Philippi when he has to say: "You are the Christ, the Son of the living God" (Matt 16:16).

If we are not ready for this final seriousness, we cannot see in Jesus more than the important founder of a religion who is worthy of human recognition, but from whom one may turn after a while to consider the founders of new religions. In countless talks about Christ it has been my experience that what stands between men and Christ is not intellectual arguments but sins. They are not willing to give up this or that. They want reservations and privileges before God. Hence they will not accept Christ as such because of the consequences. But those who want only a non–committal belief in God, which costs nothing, need not be surprised if they sit before an empty stage and miss the decisive question of their lives, the question of Christ. All so–called sympathies with Christianity are worth less than nothing to them. Those who do the will of my Father in heaven will know from whom I have my authority, whether my doctrine is of God and who I am.

We now see how far–reaching are the quiet words of Jesus. Can you not answer the question of who I am? Are you immersing yourself in the dogmas of my divine humanity, Virgin Birth and the like? Instead, do something in my name and for my sake as though I were already in your life. Try to order your life by me. Give a cup of water to the thirsty in my name. Forgive another because I have forgiven you. Surrender to me something to which you cling. Dare to lay bare your soul and become a sinner before me. Dare to let your heart be a den of thieves before me, however hard it is. Be sure that you will then suddenly think differently of me, and find a very different attitude to me, than you could ever suspect or imagine when you sought me theoretically.

Those who love him thus, who dare to love him thus, in advance, will understand the mystery of God, of the Cross, of Christmas, Good Friday and Easter.

Those who love him thus, so that it purifies their relation to others and shines out in their calling, conversation and bearing; those who in all the changes and chances of life which overthrow others can say: "Yet I am still with you;" those who can say: "I am your loving child even though your face is withdrawn for a moment and the dark curtain of mystery seems to have intervened;" those who love him with all their heart and soul and strength; those who give themselves to him and venture all on him; those who throw themselves down before him and say: "Do with me as you will, Nazarene, whoever you are, whether you are a man or the Son of God, whether you are the heart of the Father or an invented dream of human longing, here I am to be tested;" those who love him thus he will not cast out, nor will they become fools as they hope in him.

To those who love him thus he will appear as the one to whom all power is given in heaven and in earth, and they will see him as the one who has full authority to forgive sins and to break all chains.

And when he appears to me in this way, there will break from my lips a saying which I could never find by religious search, which the questioning Pharisees could not utter, but which precisely the doubting Thomas had to pronounce: "My Lord and my God!" (John 20:28).

4

The Great Mercy

One of the Pharisees asked him to eat with him, and he went into the Pharisee's house and took his place at the table. And behold, a woman of the city, who was a sinner, when she learned that he was reclining at table in the Pharisee's house, brought an alabaster flask of ointment, and standing behind him at his feet, weeping, she began to wet his feet with her tears and wiped them with the hair of her head and kissed his feet and anointed them with the ointment. Now when the Pharisee who had invited him saw this, he said to himself, "If this man were a prophet, he would have known who and what sort of woman this is who is touching him, for she is a sinner." And Jesus answering said to him, "Simon, I have something to say to you." And he answered, "Say it, Teacher."

"A certain moneylender had two debtors. One owed five hundred denarii, and the other fifty. When they could not pay, he cancelled the debt of both. Now which of them will

love him more?" Simon answered, "The one, I suppose, for whom he cancelled the larger debt." And he said to him, "You have judged rightly." Then turning toward the woman he said to Simon, "Do you see this woman? I entered your house; you gave me no water for my feet, but she has wet my feet with her tears and wiped them with her hair. You gave me no kiss, but from the time I came in she has not ceased to kiss my feet. You did not anoint my head with oil, but she has anointed my feet with ointment. Therefore I tell you, her sins, which are many, are forgiven—for she loved much. But he who is forgiven little, loves little." And he said to her, "Your sins are forgiven." Then those who were at table with him began to say among themselves, "Who is this, who even forgives sins?" And he said to the woman, "Your faith has saved you; go in peace."

Luke 7:36–50

WHAT IS A PANTOMIME? A play in which there are only actions and no words; a dumb scene. We have something of the same sort in the present story. The only speaker is Jesus himself. The main character, the sinful woman, is a dumb figure. She simply weeps and anoints the feet of Jesus. And apart from two brief formal observations none of the others present has anything to say.

Yet the whole drama is full of tension. Have you ever been a guest in the house of a strange family and suddenly they have stopped speaking? You detect that something has happened, that the atmosphere is extremely tense and that the glances cast are full of meaning. No one speaks, but a great deal happens. Everyone is full of words even though no sound is heard.

It is like that here. While Jesus speaks, taking this human

life in hand and transforming the degraded existence of this woman, the others are full of the question: How can he play the prophet? How dare he act as though he could forgive sins? Who is he anyway?

This pantomime depicts our own situation. The quiet voice of Jesus is heard in this German room of ours and no one makes open answer. He is banned from the newspapers and radio. Even in our reckoning of time he has become an anonymous figure. We no longer refer publicly to B.C. and A.D., though nevertheless he does still constitute the dividing point of world history as we reckon it. And if he is deathly silent, we cannot but feel the tension around his figure. Some accuse him. If he were a prophet, would he not have ordered these two thousand years? If he were a prophet, would not his Christians look the part? If he were a prophet, would he not come down to end injustice and to still the sea of blood and tears? Others look expectantly to his figure and know that he is the secret meaning of the darkest events and that he will finally be crowned King. They live in the name of his cross and in the shadow of his sheltering hands.

We thus see the pantomime again in our situation, even to the individual characters.

There is first the sinful woman. This woman of ill repute has dared to come into the Pharisee's house and to come to Jesus in spite of the angry glances cast at her. Vice is written on her face. The record of a wasted life may be seen in her appearance. Yet there is still something there. She has realized to the full her lost condition. She knows what is in man. She knows that man is lost. Yet she is illuminated by a gleam of hope. The glance, directed at the Nazarene, shows that here is remission and renewal, that this Jesus can be my deliverance and can transform my destiny.

Under the eyes of Jesus, therefore, she loses her fear of men. She knows that even the heads of society and leaders of the people are in final solidarity with her, the lost woman. Before this One none can boast; all must bow the knee in the dust. The man who stands under the eyes of Jesus can no longer fall victim to the veneration or worship of important men. He sees too clearly that all are guilty before this One, that the dust of mortality is on all their heads and that they are all insignificant in comparison with the inconceivable majesty of the Son of God. But, conversely, the man who stands under the eyes of Jesus can no longer fear men. He knows finally that they are flesh, that they are led against their will and that even their worst intents are under a rule of which they have no inkling. Finally, the man who stands under the eyes of Jesus can no longer despise men. He has to see them as those who are bought at great cost, for whom Jesus Christ died on the cross, and who are thus invested with the alien dignity of those for whom the Son of God suffered. He who goes to Jesus is therefore liberated from men, from their false deifications, from the fear of men and from the deadly poison of despising them.

But how does this woman come before the Son of God? The story tells us that she approaches from behind and throws herself at his feet. Her coming from behind reminds us of the solemn story in the Old Testament when Moses, hidden in a cleft of the rock, saw the Lord pass by and was then allowed to watch him from behind, since no man may see the face of the Lord and live. She approaches from behind because the eyes of the Son of God are too powerful and consuming.

We are also told that she anoints his feet in silence. There is a degree of pain which can find no words. We can see this in those who have to undergo the terrors of bombing. They first sink into a terrified silence, and only after a time can they find words to utter.

There is also a degree of awareness of guilt which has no words. "I cannot recount that of which my heart accuses me. You must take all my heart into your hands. You know it better than I do myself. I cannot say how I came to fall so low. I will not try. If only I have you! Here I am." All this is contained in the silence. The Bible uses the term "sighing" for this silent speech which can find no words. And it tells us that the Holy Spirit represents us in wordless sighing, in silent looking to God.

> *Though I have no word or cry,*
> *Do you receive my final sigh,*
> *Be gracious to me.*

While she silently does all this, she weeps to herself. And as she weeps, there takes place what always happens in weeping, whether it is external or internal. The hard crust of sorrow and guilt dissolves. (We know in the case of mourners that the worst is over when the first tears come.) And this woman can weep before Jesus. Does this soften his attitude? But who dares speak of softness when he is here enthroned in royal independence of men and dares not merely protect a prostitute but cause her to sit with him? Yet although he has this kingly severity and superiority, he has the kindness to let her weep. He is always the one in whose proximity our griefs dissolve. Jesus is the one place in the world were we need not restrain our sorrows because he already knows them all.

These tears before the Son of God, however, are a special kind. They are not the tears of a wailing woman. They arise from proximity to Jesus. Everything brought into proximity to Jesus is changed and sanctified. This shows itself in the fact that her tears are tears of joy. The gesture of anointing is an indication of this joy, of this uplift of spirit. She is like a child lost in the dark forest of life but now found by its mother and enclosed in her arms. All the anxiety, the distress of conscience, pours out. But the child is already at home and its mother understands. This is how it always is with us men. We are all like children in the dark forest. But we do not pour out our secret anxiety and impotence. We perhaps whistle and put on an outward show. But when we come to Jesus we see for the first time the full terror of the wood in which we have been.

It always seems to me to be one of the greatest things about Jesus that he allows us to realize all the terrors of guilt and death only when we are at home and safe in him. Nothing shakes us so severely as the Sermon on the Mount. But is it not very significant that this disclosure of the thoughts of our hearts does not take place until Jesus is present? And do not the depths look very different in the light of the Savior because he speaks words of supreme comfort as well as terror?

All this is, of course, concealed from the spectators and guests. They do not realize that someone is coming home. They do not see that a little ship is reaching harbor. They see only the external side, the façade which is what we always see of one another. They perhaps think: "The dreadful extravagance of the woman to fall at the feet of Jesus and anoint him!" They think: "What liberties men take with this Nazarene!" The same thoughts recur in the later story of the community: "Is it not extravagant, fantastic, mad, that they let themselves be imprisoned and tortured and killed for him when they could far more easily avoid a decision with a little compromise? Does it not pass comprehension that face to face with the wild beasts in the arena they praise him, singing 'Jesus my Joy' even as they perish?"

Simon the Pharisee shakes his head when he sees the conduct of this sinful woman. So, too, many spectators of the drama of Christ and the martyrs shake their heads. "I have no need to act like that," thinks Simon. "I do not understand it. My faith is quite different. I know what I should do; I know who God is; I know where I am going after death. This is sober religion. There is no need to act like that."

Jesus knows what he is thinking. "Yes, you are very sober," he answers indirectly. "You did nothing when I arrived. You did not provide water to wash my feet. You did not give me a kiss or a welcome. You did not anoint my head with oil. You tread your way of rectitude, Simon. You act justly, you harm nobody. You do not need to make any religious display. But do you not see why this woman is so very different in her greeting and cannot restrain herself from joy and praise?" He then tells Simon the parable of the two debtors. The one has been forgiven much, the other little. It is obvious who will be the more grateful.

Simon must then have seen, as I hope we see, why the sinful woman makes that extravagant gesture of anointing. She is like the debtor whose gigantic debt has been canceled. She knows the greatness of her guilt, and she thus bows low at the feet of the Savior and dares not meet his eyes. It is only because she has this self–knowledge that she sees the full glory of this figure of the Savior. She resembles Isaiah, who was aware of the uncleanness of his lips and who could thus estimate the full greatness of the appearance of God in the temple. She is like Peter, who knew that he was a sinful man and who for that reason saw in Jesus the Son of God. She sees the divine element in Jesus before others, even before those for whom religion is a vocation; and she does so because she is led to a frontier where alone she can go no further and knows herself to be lost.

How many of us have been led to this frontier?—to a sorrow in which we are imprisoned as in a steel cage, to a guilt which pursues us in the night and disturbs our conscience, to a frontier where God refuses his comfort. Later we have learned to regard these hours as the most blessed in our lives. We have suddenly learned the truth of the hymns which speak of the coming of powerful help in time of greatest need. But would I have ever seen this without the hours of helplessness and darkness? We can sympathize with those who have not been brought to this frontier of extreme poverty. They are the poorer in encounters with eternity. And they finally suppose that they themselves are eternal and that everything revolves around their petty life and significance. We can see this at their table. Jesus is as near to them as breathing. He has entered their house, as with so many of us who have behind us a Christian upbringing and instruction in the Christian religion. But the men in the dining room of Simon are too self-confident, too full of their own virtue and excellence, to be open to the glory of the Son of God who seeks to encounter them. The poor woman, however, sits in the dark well of guilt and sorrow, and she can thus see the light which suddenly rises on the firmament of her poor life. We have to become little to see the greatness of God. We have to be impotent to descry his miracles. We have to know our guilt to understand the secret of his holiness and forgiving goodness.

May the sorrowful among us, who have come to that frontier and sit in such depths, realize that Jesus wills to bless and sanctify these bitter hours, indeed, to make them creative! May they see that they are not in a prison of the body from which there is no escape, but in a house to which Jesus comes! They have only to look up and to be ready to let him sanctify their tears.

Then they will see him through these tears as the Brother and Companion of their sorrow, as the Saviour from the depths. If we have not cried to him from the depths, we have not cried to him at all; we know nothing of the secret of prayer. The most blessed hours of life are not those we spend on sunlit heights; they are the hours of pain in the depths if only these hours are spent under the eyes of Jesus.

A further point which emerges from the parable of the debtors is that the woman loves the Savior so passionately because the whole mountain of her guilt has suddenly been removed. Her thanksgiving is like that of a criminal who see his death sentence torn up. She rejoices like a prisoner whose chains are taken off. What is expressed in her extravagant gesture is the whole joy of liberation. Everything suddenly looks different. The world is seen to be the place where Jesus accomplishes his great work and Christmas has come. Men look different because they can no longer be feared, despised or deified, but are to be loved as brothers of this Lord. The living God has lost his aspects of terror and consuming fire, for he has become our Father through Christ.

Do we understand this mysterious saying of Jesus: "He who is forgiven much, loves much"? The woman was not a strict churchwoman. She knew no dogmas. She could not engage in theological discussion. But she had the love of those who sit in the depths and who suddenly perceive the hand of deliverance.

How many of us are perhaps correctly instructed about Jesus, first–class students of religion, zealous readers of the Bible or profound investigators! But possibly we do not have the love of this great sinner. Yet this is the only thing which counts with Jesus. For dealings with Christ are not a matter of the intellect and of enquiry. They are a matter of life, and of the eyes from which it must speak. Hence the bitterest accusation ever made against Christians is the saying of Nietzsche: "You must look more redeemed to me if I am to believe in your Redeemer."

Alongside the sinful woman we must now consider the Pharisee. He is marked by two features.

First, he will believe in the Son of God only if he corresponds to his own wishful thinking about him, and therefore only if God dances to his tune. The conditional statements he makes are typical: "If this man were a prophet, he would know what kind of woman this is." He is one of the If–men we are always meeting. If God will save me from this situation, I will believe in him. If God will treat me as I desire, I will believe in him. If, if, if.... And because the Pharisee lays down these conditions for God, he fails to see that God has actually crossed his way in Christ. The woman, on the other hand, does not speak to Jesus. She makes no conditions. But she listens the more attentively to what he says. And she is ready to be corrected and apprehended by him to the very depths of her heart and mind.

Secondly, the Pharisee thinks of God as his debtor. He presents his account; he has always acted justly and never harmed anyone. This is typical of us men. God is almost always our debtor. He has to pay us according to our own self–assessment. He owes us for the grief we have to bear, for the way he directs history and sends sun and wind, rain and storms, upon our crops. So long as we assign to God no more than the part of a factor in the life program which we arbitrarily propose for ourselves, he cannot meet us; for God is no mere factor. Nor can we receive true comfort even when we open the Bible or listen to sermons. It is worth noting that so long as we cry: "Tell us, God, why you do this or that; explain, that we may be comforted," we never find comfort. It is only when we learn to be silent and to say:

"We are not God's creditors, he does not owe us anything; on the contrary, God is our Creditor and we can only submit to him for grace or judgment," that we really come to know his divine comfort.

God does not have to answer us. We have to answer to God. And we cannot do so. The most we can say is: "Depart from me, for I am a sinful man." It is this most painful moment, the moment of empty hands, which will become the moment of grace. God loves empty hands and hungering hearts and a contrite spirit.

Hence we should call this story that of one who was greatly blessed rather than the story of the great sinner. We are not to say that it deals with the disintegration of a human life but more accurately that it deals with attainment to the shores of a new life's day. This woman is thus the epitome of Christian life generally.

This life may be described from two angles. The longer we are in the presence of Jesus, the more deeply we know our sin and the sharper our conscience. This being so, we plunge ever deeper into debt with God. Those who know the Christian life only from outside find it hard to understand that the longer a Christian is with Christ the deeper his indebtedness, so that he can never leave the school of Christ as a completed and accomplished graduate free from all faults or omissions. But because this is so, and we increasingly realize our guilt in the light of Jesus, we have an increasing love for the One who wills to be the Savior of our life. He who is forgiven much, loves much. Theologians have constantly debated whether there is development or progress in the Christian life. Does not fellowship with Jesus necessarily bring growth? Or is the Christian state complete from the very first? Is sin forgiven once for all? Is there no progress beyond it? Well, there is surely a kind of divine school in which we move up from class to class. There is surely development and growth in the Christian life. Yet we must not think of this progress in terms of our always becoming more holy and blameless. If we fall into this error, serious reverses will bring us back to soberness and a salutary anxiety.

We may, however, come to love him more and more—and this is perhaps the true progress of the Christian life. Indeed, it undoubtedly is. And this progress in love does not mean that our soul acquires an increasing ability to love. It rests on the fact that we are increasingly forgiven. The more Jesus Christ humbles us, the greater our joy and the more jubilant our thanks. We do not increase before God. His goodness increases, and it is for this reason that we love him more. "I must decrease, but he must increase." This can be said only by great sinners, by those at the frontier. The last words of Luther after his great Christian life were not: "Look, Lord, how much I have progressed in love for you. For your sake I have known the greatest distress of conscience, the deepest loneliness and supreme achievement. Now you must open heaven to me." Luther did not speak in such terms. His last words were simply: "We are beggars, that is true."

But do you not think that God heard rather more in this dying confession than merely that we are beggars? Do you not think that in heaven he heard the unspoken accompanying statement: "Therefore you know, O God, how greatly I must love you"?

> *Nothing of myself I bring,*
> *You, O God, are everything*

Do you think that he heard this statement too?

5

Vicarious Intercession

WE ARE IMPRESSED AND MOVED by the fact that countless millions are not reached by our preaching, that they cannot be brought within physical distance of our summons. Even when one of the great churches of our cities is full to bursting, a sober assessment forces us to agree that we touch only one sector of the city with our message. The Church in these days prior to the return of its Lord seems to be built, like the hut of Philemon and Baucis, in a land which is far from God. Yet no less has happened than that the kingdom of God has come among us.

This situation is felt particularly by our soldiers and theologians in the services. They live and march with innumerable comrades to whom they are bound by battle, terror and joy. They know what God has done for them all. They know that Christ has died for them. Yet they see thousands miss this decisive point in their destiny. They see that they overlook eternity for the daily routine. They know and see these things, and they pray that at least the stones of history will cry out and testify when they must be silent or can only speak in brief and lonely discussions of that which shakes the world because it is grounded in eternity. For the light of this witness can light up the faces only of the closest companions. The majority, who deep down also have a great longing, remain in darkness. What real Christian does not feel the pang which Jesus himself knew when he saw the multitude as sheep without a shepherd! And conversely who of us does not know the sorrow of the shepherd without a flock! Yet whatever God sends us is not designed to make us mourn and complain. All that God sends is creative and positive. It sets us a task. It sets us before this task. For good or evil, therefore, we must ask what task God is setting us through this pang in our soul. I believe that it is the task of the intercessor. I am not thinking now of mere prayer requests. I mean vicarious intercession.

This thought has been strangely neglected theologically, though it might well be adapted to open up entirely new vistas in prayer. If I were to describe it briefly I should put it as follows. The important thing for our people, and for the whole restless and inattentive world, is not the content of this intercession. It is the simple fact that such intercession is made within it. What matters is the sheer existence of those who pray. It is not without significance for a people that there should be in it a little band of those who bear up the whole nation vicariously in their prayers. It is not without significance for a people that in it baptism should be given, prayer offered and the Lord's Supper administered, even though the majority neither hear nor understand.

Scripture itself gives us not a few concealed hints at the vicarious existence of those who pray, at the presence of this little company. One such hint is to be seen negatively in the absence of the ten righteous in Sodom and Gomorrah (Genesis 18:16ff), who, if they had been present, would have been able to change the destiny of this world in microcosm. These disturbing ten might not have had opportunity to preach in the overpowering flood of ungodliness. They might not have been able to change the destiny of their world by their message. But they would have been present before God; and because of the intercession of Abraham this would have been enough—vicarious representation.

Does not Jesus direct us along the same lines when, speaking of the demonic derangement and final tribulations of history, he says of the vicarious existence of his community: "And if the Lord had not cut short the days, no human being would be saved. But for the sake of the elect, whom he chose, he shortened the days" (Mark 13:20)? We might also refer to the curious saying of the apostle Paul about baptism for the dead, in which men undergo baptism for those already dead to incorporate them vicariously into their own baptism (1 Corinthians 15:29). A. Schlatter is strongly against the view that this is to be decried as a superstition, since we know very little of the historical background of the practice and we ourselves have been responsible for other innovations at this point. In the reference to baptism for the dead he sees an indication of the fact that the existence of a man of blessing and prayer cannot be without significance for his family, nation and friends. Paul says quite explicitly that in a mixed marriage the unbelieving partner is sanctified by the believing, and even the children are taken up into the stream of blessing which flows from the believing parent (1 Corinthians 7:14).

It seems to me that these ideas are continually finding unconscious expression in the letters and reports of our soldiers. How often we read: Our spiritual life is withering in the everlasting monotony, in the full round of everyday duties, in the inner isolation. Therefore pray for us, intercede for us before God, let us be taken up into the fellowship of praying people even though our own voice is silent and almost extinguished.

This urgent request implies more than that we should merely make them the object of our prayers. There is the more profound appeal: Even though I myself drop out as a subject of prayer, you take my place before God. Act for me when my own heart and senses are pressed by duties or choked by the dust of the interminable way. Or am I mistaken if I think I detect this appeal for vicarious intercession in letters from the front line, both military and ecclesiastical, with its thousands in posts of isolation? If I am not mistaken, then we must ask how we are to evaluate the experience.

For there are many who write that it is a comfort to them that services are being held and prayers being offered, namely, that the Church is doing something vicariously for them, even while they themselves do not participate.

Two other factors seem to me to point in the same direction. First, it is to be noted that even the most secularized of men, who hardly ever hear the Word, would not like to see the Church obliterated even though they themselves make no use of it. Indeed, if the faith and confessions of the Church seem to be attacked, they close the ranks as if they were under the cross around which they merely stand as spectators. How are we to explain this contradiction? Obviously many secularized people do not want the intercession of the Church, its influencing of the course of the world prayer, to stop. In the stress of their own pilgrimage they at least stretch out a little finger to grasp the horns of the altar by whose vicarious existence they

wish to be sheltered. A completely non–Christian teaching col-
league at a summer educational camp once said to me: "When
you meet the good Lord, greet him from me, and ask him not to
trip me because I have not been to see him for some time." For
those who have ears to hear, this typically veiled and flippant
approach of the worldling conveys an appeal for the vicarious
intercession of the Christian who, he believes, has some knowledge of the ultimate realities and who has contact with them in
prayer. In other words, it is not unimportant whether the hut
and sacred grove of Philemon and Baucis are near to the pal-
ace of the emperor or not. Goethe was certainly thinking along
these lines in the relevant scene in *Faust.*

Do not all of us who call ourselves Christians, perhaps in a
mass meeting or in the busiest traffic of a main street, suddenly have the thought sometimes: Into what abyss are all these
people pouring with their passions, doubts, and hopes written
on their faces, riveted to the moment and forgetful of eternity? And you scurry like one of thousands of ants among them,
among these brother men—you who alone know that God is
seeking them all and yourself; you who are like a sober man in
an intoxicated world. Therefore you must intercede for them
all before God; you must be one whose hands are stretched out
to and over them. Like the ten righteous, then ten justified, we
must represent before God all those who do not know what
they are doing and do not do what they know.

Secondly, we remember that in Romans 8 Paul speaks of the
sighing and longing of the creation and that he has in view the
non–human sphere of creaturely life. How, then, can we understand the petition: "Your Kingdom come," except in the sense
that we are to include in our request for the coming kingdom
irrational nature, its suffering and savage strife, the demonic

nature of its enslavement and its chaotic and tumultuous disorder? But if this is so, our prayer again has a vicarious function in which we are spokesmen for this dumb and irrational creation, praying for the kingdom of God on its behalf, that nature should be redeemed as well as history and that the new heaven and the new earth should absorb it, too, into its totality. From every angle, I believe, we are led to this thought of vicarious representation, and it is one of the obscure graces of God in this time of affliction that we should learn it from our sufferings.

Naturally, we cannot speak of it responsibly without mentioning the dangers. To quote an expression of Kähler, I might say that the dangers lie especially in "exclusive substitution." By this I mean the vicarious representation which absolves others from personal decision because I illegitimately take it upon myself. We see this to some extent in the Roman Catholic doctrine of implicit faith, by which the Church believes representatively for me. If we interpret vicarious representation in this way, we misuse it not only in self–deification but also and supremely in evasion of the decision of confession. We shun the duty of proclamation and choose the easier way of prayer. But as faith without works is dead, so prayer is dead without the work of proclamation. Vicarious intercession must not become a cloak for wickedness, in this case quietism. Vicarious intercession springs from love; and love impels to proclamation rather than dispenses with it. Substitution is either inclusive or it is a deception.

If, then, we are pointed to vicarious intercession from so many angles, we need to rethink our prayers in the light of it.

Again, I can refer only to the essential points. Two questions arise. One of these is obvious, but the other may seem strange to those who have no experience of the truth concerned. In our public prayers, do we not push into the background our petition for those who have not come, not so much in protest but in sheer alienation? I am thinking now of something far more basic and serious than such summary requests as that God may shake the self–confident. As the objects of this prayer I am thinking of brother men who fail to hear the truth of God, not because of self–confidence, but because of physical remoteness. It is this world which is "out of hearing" that we who know and intercede should represent. Part of the inner demonism of our aeon is that from time to time it gives rise to periods when we have to accept the fact of this world which is "out of hearing" and cannot proclaim our message. And it is precisely in these periods, when salvation is concealed, the markets are closed and "worshippers are hidden in the cathedral" (Reinhold Schneider), that the community of knowledge is called to intercession and vicarious representation. In prayer, the heads of believers may be hidden almost to the point of invisibility and inaudibility; but in this concealment they pray.

In individual prayer—for we cannot do this publicly—do we so take the needs of men to ourselves that we literally pray in their names instead of merely for them, daring to say: "Our Father..." in the first person, in their first person, so that they are the subjects? We can dare to do this only when we have shared particular experiences with specific people; but when we have, we should not fail to do it.

The strongest actualization of vicarious representation will always, of course, be the daring exception. The theological place for it seems to me to be much the same as that of sponsors using the "I" form in the name of infants at baptism. Here the infant is taken as a member of the community in which it must grow to maturity. Until it does so, the community acts vicariously for it in the inclusive sense. Is there any stronger or more impressive commitment of sponsors than this substitutionary I, which we have tended to abandon together with vicarious intercession? In the light of it, can a sponsor go away from the service well satisfied that he has done his duty? Does not this substitutionary I blind him to the infant in an unheard of and absolutely obligatory way, just because he has dared vicarious representation of baptism, and also of intercession!

With these brief remarks we are simply opening a new door into the vast chamber of our commission to pray; we are simply helping to win for the office of prayer a new task and a new promise. In this task even those who are isolated or who cannot speak may find work to do before God. From the great unrest of those who are apparently useless they are called back to the rest and peace which are given by the consciousness of service, of a service by which the world is to be delivered. The man who prays thus is called, with nine others, to save the city. This is his ministry, his work, his joy.

6

On the Threshold of the Future

*And it shall come to pass, when I bring a cloud over
the earth, that the bow shall be seen in the cloud.*

Genesis 9:14, KJV

WE ALL KNOW THE BACKGROUND of this text. The catastrophe of the flood had overwhelmed the godless and
self–destructive world. Only a feeble ark and those inside it
had escaped. These few survivors are extremely lonely in the
waste of the vast and silent world slowly emerging from the
fatal deluge.

Recently an illustrated paper has dealt with the question of
the possible destruction of the world through the unleashing
of atomic energy. The pictures portray realistically the terrible
storms and cloudbursts, the mass killings through radioactive
dust and the mountainous waves engulfing whole continents.
And the accompanying article speaks of a few survivors left
alone in a frightening silence in which the words and songs of

men are stilled, the birds no longer sing and the eyes are terrified by the spectacle of hopeless and helpless destruction. It is thus the men around Noah, the very last to remain alive, must have contemplated the horrors of a drowned world. This was surely the end.

But against all expectation the goodness of God is not yet at an end even when men are and even when the world has been brought to the destruction of the flood.

In spite of all appearances to the contrary, God still has a plan for this bankrupt world. He still has something in store for it. This dark, satanic earth, drowned in blood and tears, this earth of ours, he still wants as a theatre for his grace and glorious direction. To be sure, there will still be thunder and lightning about us. We have no promise that our earth will be a paradise. We have no promise that reason will always prevail or that men will be angels. If we believe this, we do not get it from the Bible but from pipe dreams or the clouds. What we can believe is that all that happens, however dreadful, will carry with it God's blessing. His gracious, hidden hand will be with us. Above all the terrors which engulf us will stand the gracious ark of his mercy.

We ourselves at the end of the present year also belong to this landscape between the evening of a drowned world and the morning of a new day, to this landscape after the flood. Like the people of the ark, we have survived the dreadful storms, and we can now survey the ruins from Mount Ararat.

We think of the loved ones who have gone from us, perhaps on deathbeds or in the terror of battles or bombing. We remember those whom the storms have scattered to remote corners, our prisoners at the ends of the earth who this evening are looking out through the barbed wire to the dawning New Year with eager eyes of longing, carrying in their hearts the anxious question whether the hand of God will really be stronger than the enemy fist which pitilessly grasps and keeps them.

We think of all those who sigh in prison without trial, or condemned by false trial, and who lift a quivering finger to ask whether in this world of victors and vanquished, of despotism and slavery, there is any righteous God, and if so whether he is doing anything for them.

We think of the silent bells of a home we have lost and of the extinguished candles of a vanished childhood. We think of the people, and especially the children, who will be greeting the New Year in damp and gloomy bunkers, of the old folk who face ruin through currency reform, of brothers and sisters behind the Iron Curtain who all have a question to put to the New Year.

It is indeed a great darkness which surrounds us on the frontier of this year. And the time which beats and roars so strongly on the shore of this New Year's Eve forces us to ask whether all these living people whom we love are not being engulfed and destroyed by this rushing stream of time, whether time does not flow on without them, covering their traces and spreading a great silence over them. Have we really to write off all these who hunger for life and righteousness, for home and security? "The stars above and the graves below are still"—but a great cry goes up between the unfeeling silence of the firmament and the night of death.

To be sure, we must not forget the other aspect of our destiny on this last night of the year. For our time still goes on. We have escaped. We are spared. In relation to the past we may sing of the many situations in which the gracious God has spread his wings about us. How many of us rejoice that we have work to do in the New Year! How many of us are only too ready to put a hand to the wheel to lift the car out of the mud! How many of us have to give thanks for the powers which God has given us and for helpers on the way! But on every hand this stammering praise is encircled by the dark questions which oppress us.

There is also a question ahead. Inevitably on this threshold of the year we look to the future and ask what the coming year may bring. I think our text has something to say about this forward look, since it is specifically addressed to the survivors, to those who still have the terrors of the catastrophes in their bones, who still see the glare of destruction and hear the gurgle of the engulfing waters, but who nevertheless, by the mercy of God, have now been set on a new path.

Luther's translation indicates in the opening words the mystery of the future: "If it shall come...." In relation to the coming year we ask, do we not, what will come. On the threshold of a New Year we are undoubtedly in danger of falling victim to an optical illusion, as when we are in a stationary train and another train parallel to us begins to move. It seems as though we are moving and the other train is stationary, that it is an immobile, unending stretch on which we advance, rapidly moving into the New Year. But is not this the very opposite of the truth? Are we really crossing the threshold of the New Year? Is not the New Year itself crossing the threshold and coming to us? The future (*Zukunft*) is that which comes to us (*zukommt*). And it is because deep down we know this that we ask what the New Year will bring us, what it will bring with it and carry to us.

This is the suggestion of the text: "If it shall *come* to pass...." Indeed, something is coming. And Scripture tells us that it will be clouds. It does not tell us what clouds, nor where the lightning will strike. It simply says that something, an unknown x,

will come. What the text denotes is the plentitude of the possibilities which worry us by their very indefiniteness, by the
yawning gulf of "it." Perhaps the lightning will flame between
the continents, between East and West. Perhaps this is the "it"
which shall come. Perhaps all that I have built today will be
swept away tomorrow. Or perhaps the "it" will be something
very different. Perhaps the love which I have for someone else,
and which is happily returned, will grow cold, and the moment
of bliss which I should like to tarry will pitilessly fade. Will this
be the "it?" (How many of us live in panic lest doors should
close like this!) Perhaps my husband will remain in prison or
will be finally missing. Or perhaps he will return and be different. Is this the "it?" But then—we can never enumerate all the
possibilities. We can only try to realize what is meant by the
dark saying: "If it shall come to pass...." For something is coming. I may have no specific fear. My life may take a fairly regular
course. But life is so incalculable and the future is so obscure.
Even if I have no particular fear, I often worry about the very
indefiniteness of the future. In such cases we speak of fear of
life. But it is here that the text offers us royal consolation and
encouragement. For God says: "I am the one who causes the
clouds to pass over the earth." Hence what is at work is not a
blind "it" of fate or chance. A hand is stretched over the clouds,
and it is this, and this alone, which assigns to cloud and air and
wind their path and course. All things, therefore, will turn out
for good. For the hand which is here at work is the same hand
which for us allowed itself to be pierced and nailed to the cross;
it is the same hand which rested in blessing on the heads of the
children and which healed tortured bodies; it is the same hand
which stretches forth in majesty and can command the wind

and the waves, so that the lake instantly becomes a silver mirror and the storm a requickening breath.

Lo, this is the hand at work when the storms rage, and nothing can happen but what this good hand controls, having already experienced and tested it to see that it is good for us.

> *For nothing can befall,*
> *But he has seen it all,*
> *And we can call it blessed.*

For this reason, Christians can always face the future with confidence. And because they look for this hand, they can finally be indifferent to what is brewing outside and what will come. They know no more than others what will come. But they do know who will come.

The comforting royal vision of the seer of Patmos is like this. He sees the clouds of the Last Day gathering over history. The end of all things, the triumphant divine victory, is intimated by clouds and terrors. On these clouds, however, there does not ride the flaming chariot of the avenging angel. On these clouds there comes the King, Jesus Christ, and his final advent dawns.

Whatever comes, whatever good or ill the coming year may bring, will bring us to maturity and prepare us for this final royal moment. To go towards this is the final meaning of history, or your life and mine. If we keep this in view, we can go confidently through the storms with sure steps, for we may know that all the cracks and rolls around us are simply the echoing thunder of the tempest in which Satan is cast down from heaven and which accompanies the great victory of Christ over all the forces that tried to wrest us from the hand of God and to rob us of the peace of the children of God. We may indeed say:

Though sin and hell are round us,
Jesus will surround us.

Thus the shadow in which we must walk during the coming year is not finally the shadow of the dark and dangerous clouds, but of his loving and powerful hand.

This means that world history, as illustrated by the monumental stories of the Bible, is fitted and held together by the first rainbow which shone over the catastrophe of the flood and the end of the primitive world, and also by the second rainbow which John the Divine saw around the throne of God before which world history will some day end. Certainly, the path taken by this history is dark. It leads past precipices and under storms. We have come to realize this, and will do so even more in the future. Nevertheless, this path begins in the name of a great love which is faithful to this distracted world, and it ends in a great consummation, namely, at the precise point where God would have us all, Russians and Americans, prisoners in Siberia and mothers in Altersheim, children yet to be born and the dead in distant seas.

Truly, we are not journeying into the void. Though we are blinded by cloud and lightning, everything is infinitely different from what we think. The hymn speaks of the reality:

I journey in the way,
And home will be my goal,
Where more than I can say,
My Father will console.

In spite of every appearance to the contrary, our way does in fact lead from God's gracious bow at the beginning to his triumphant bow at the end. We may rest in the heart of God and find shelter in his omnipotent might.

This leads us to the second point which our text proclaims to our comfort. God will always let us see his gracious and triumphant bow when life goes hard. Have we ever noticed how a rainbow arises? The sun suddenly breaks through the clouds with magical brilliance even though the elements are still raging and their wildness has not been allayed. And now notice a strange feature, namely, that light never celebrates such a riot of color as when it breaks up into spectrum. And this festival of light takes place at the very moment when the rays of the sun, of the sun of divine grace, clash with the raging elements of our earth.

We understand what is implied in the image. It is precisely in grief and pain, in the depths and under the storms, that God will show himself and display before us the fulness of his grace. Do you understand this? Do you understand it precisely when you consider your own life? Like myself, you can probably attest it with thanksgiving only when it has all proved true, and will again prove true, in your own life. Have you ever detected his consoling presence so clearly as when you were delivered up to the most terrible distress where no shelter could save you from the attack, no doctor help you and no man speak to you a word of real comfort?

The bow always shines with greatest comfort in times of darkness, and it is in the depths that God's hand is stretched out with the greatest love. If only we see this we will believe God's promise. Thus the bow of mercy overarches the coming year too. It will not be only a year of terror. It will be also a year of indescribable consolations because it will be a year of the Lord, who awaits us with his miracles. At exactly the right moment a helping word will come as his messenger. His love will encounter us in a man whom he sends, or in a child who smiles at us, or in a wonderful confirmation, or in a liberating prayer which he enables us to utter and in which he takes from us our cares like a father. Since we have a Father, we are not adventurers. We are those who live by the surprises and miracles of their God.

Thus we stand on this threshold of the two years consoled and thankful and full of cheerful hope. God gives us a further span of time, and all things may again become new. For the final message of our text is that we may cast behind us our past, the old year with its guilt and failures and sins, burying it in the depths of the eternal mercy. The rainbow was the sign that a new world was to begin and that God will give us another chance. Hence we are not to be the servants of our past and its guilt. God has cancelled it. His Son has taken it upon himself and borne it away. There is to be a new beginning. Do you realize what it means that we can begin again from the beginning, that God has obliterated the past, that he has wiped out our debts? Christians are men with a future. The burden of their past has been lifted. They are free, and they live by forgiveness. God's radiant bow is simply the heavenly writ of forgiveness and a new beginning.

Thus the night of the past year with its guilt may really be past in the name of God; the rainbow shines and will give a new day. The morning will break, and his mercy has no end but is new every morning and his faithfulness is great.

"We bid you hope"—this verse from Goethe's creed has acquired for us Christians a new, triumphant and festal sense.

Let us then be of good courage as we go into this New Year. We are people with a future because we belong to the One who will arise and come on his day. Over the dark valleys through which we must go rise up the mountains from which our help comes, and the flush of the coming glory already touches their summits. No lightning can strike us; there is only flashing and rumbling, the paths are prepared and smoothed on which our feet may tread; they are prepared by the One who ascribes to the winds and storms their course. And everywhere the surprises of God are waiting for us. Blessed are the eyes which may see what it is promised that you shall see.

> *Lightnings all around us play,*
> *Be Thou all our strength and stay...*
> *Through the darkness of the night,*
> *Lead, O lead, eternal light!*

PART TWO

Festival Sermons

7

The Message of Redeeming Light (Christmas)

There the eternal light breaks through,
All the world doth shine anew;
Bright its radiance in the night,
To make us children of the light.

IF WE TAKE LIGHT SERIOUSLY, we have also to reckon with the fact that there is a night in which it shines. This is the limit of all Christmas dreams. These dreams can be a danger because our closed eyes no longer notice when the true light shines from without.

Naturally men crowd into the magic circle of the Christmas light, whether dreamed, invented or authentic. They all come out of the drabness of shadowed spheres to be merry for a while in this light—the cold and hungry, the inmates of underground shelters and other places of refuge, the outcast, homeless and lonely, the most pitiable with the illusions of their distorted minds—they all come to forget for a moment, to drown their memories, to enjoy a happy moment of distraction, like the chorus of prisoners in Beethoven's Fidelio, from whom the streaming sunshine over the prison yard evokes a song of yearning, causing them to forget the dungeon for an hour of dreaming.

Forgetfulness of the darkness, however, can make us cheerful only for a short while in an imagined light, because this light is not understood as a miracle. It is a miracle only if night is taken seriously—the darkness which lies over the earth and the nations, the shadow of death in which we all sit, the nightly ghost of care and the daily apparition of fear, and above all the sinister enslavement to guilt.

Only when we accept all this, and do so in the hard and unconditional form of being ready to see it in the particular and biographically demonstrable aspects which this darkness takes on in our lives, can we appreciate the miracle of the fact that God has broken into it all, that he has torn heaven open and released a flood of light on the earth in an undeniable event of change and renewal. Cannot even the remains of destroyed cities look like havens of greenery, and shattered ruins acquire an aura of romance when the sunshine transforms them in the magic of its glow?

But this comparison bids us pause. We have been diverted for a moment by what is usually conveyed to us by the term "light" and we have allowed our imagination to pursue it. Perhaps we had to do so in order to grasp how different is the light proclaimed in the Christmas message.

For would it really be a redeeming light if it merely shone magically over the ruins of this aeon, deceptively blurring the contours of meaninglessness and giving to them a softer outline? Would not the brief enchantment necessarily yield again to the harsh and sober reality which shows the dream to be a mirage and which is ashamed of its falsity?

And if we are to construe in general terms our image of God opening heaven and causing his light to shine on the earth, it may well be asked where this light is when the nations are at war or glare at one another in mistrust. Does it shine on cemeteries old and new? Does it shine in iron cages or on deserts which were once fertile fields?

It is here that we see the difference between the Christmas message of light and our human ideas. For we are not now concerned with visible space and a supra–temporal and, as it were, omnipresent radiance. We have to grasp the unusual and difficult thought that all heaven is indeed opened, that all the fulness of the light of eternity streams down, that all the angels and heavenly choirs are assembled at this point of irruption, that they permeate the heavenly radiance with their song of praise, and yet that this incursion of eternity which fulfills all hope and longing is concentrated at a single point, namely, where the child lies in its crib, where the love of God is so big that it gives itself in what is smallest, where the eternity of God is so mighty that it enters a feeble and despised body. For its strength is not in size and greatness. It is its ability to give itself, to become small, in order to draw near to those who are poor and needy and who can never storm heaven of themselves.

"There the eternal light breaks through"—that is, only where the poor infant is. The stress is on the "there." And we must be on our way if we are to find the infant there and to become there "children of the light." But we no longer need to try to lift ourselves out of the endless dungeons of this dark world. Our forces are weak, and any substitute achievement of the imagination which we might proclaim is an illusion. We no longer need it. For the light itself has come down and it shines through the pit. We must go to the place where it meets the bottom and comes into the most secret and troubled recesses of our lives. Precisely "there" God will meet us. Precisely "there" the Son waits for us.

We cannot sink so low that God is not lower. For the descent of the Christmas child did not reach its lowest point on Christmas night. It was perhaps reached when the Crucified cried out: "My God, my God, why have you forsaken me?" This most terrible affliction, in which Jesus did not merely suffer his own torment of body and soul but also bore the alien guilt and pain of infinite times and places and hosts, lies beyond the extreme limit which can be reached by human suffering. No depth of human agony cannot be brought into the span between the crib and the cross, where it is taken and enclosed by nail–pierced hands.

We cannot lay too strong an emphasis, then, on the fact that Christmas does not describe a state of general transfiguration but rather an event at a specific historical point to which we must go if we are to stand in this light.

Two further thoughts will perhaps help to make this clear.

There is a popular but not a truly Christian hymn which misses the comfort of Christmas by singing of the home of the soul which is up above in light. In other words, we are not pointed to the Christmas scene with the child, the shepherds, and the angelic choirs above the stall. We are referred to an imaginary scene in which our bodies are walking prisons and above which is the heavenly sphere in inaccessible radiance, the object of the tired longing of resignation.

Here, however, everything is very different. The eternal God has left the heavenly glory and chosen the poor manger as his home. He has placed himself with us in the prison of anxiety and care, the temptation and sorrow, which can afflict only a son of earth.

After this demonstration of divine love, we can no longer be hypnotized by the brutality of this world. We have love even in our hovel and ruins. This poor tortured earth has provided a manger and a cross to be the home of the Son of God. Hence it can no longer be wholly alien to us. It has become a fore-taste of the eternal home which came into this far country of ours in that time of salvation. Now that the light has broken through the dark dungeons of anxiety and confusion, it cannot be totally dark, for there is a companion in the dark valley and the signal of the divine world shows us which way to take in our pilgrimage.

Even this poor earth has its share of the radiance of this alien righteousness and dignity now that the crib and the cross have been set up in it and it has been blessed by the grace which it could not attain of itself. For it is now no longer held fast in its own torment. It has become the bearer of signs which point beyond itself to the promise which is no longer of this world but which is given to this world.

Another new factor as compared with all that we men think we know and venture to imagine as light is as follows.

During the night we console ourselves with thoughts of the dawn, and during winter we wait for the spring which will awaken new life. The eternal rhythm of nature is our comfort.

Here, however, we have a darkness over the earth and the nations from which there is no escape. Here is the night in which no man can work. Here the imagination of wickedness gives itself to increasingly terrible excesses until the day of judgment. Here is war and tumult which can never end in the happiness of eternal peace but even at best can only be interrupted by brief and illusory armistices.

Nor are we told that in the engulfing night we are to wait for the day. For this will never come, in spite of fools who expect a social and political paradise. What we are told with reference to the Christmas light is: "Bright its radiance in the night."

Even now, as we sit in chaos, the peace of God is proclaimed to us. Even now the angels sing. Even now God intimates to us the presence of his love and his miracles.

And have we not all tasted something of it? Which have been our most happy hours? Have they not been the hours in the depths, in the night from which there is no escape, rather than the moments of joy in which we have rejoiced for a short time in some light or other, like butterflies? There is, of course, no psychological law that sorrow has a greater power of purgation than joy. Many have been broken by sorrow. It has been to them a curse rather than a blessing. Here, however, the mystery of the kingdom of God is manifest, namely, that God has come into the depth to seek us and that the light shines in the darkness. It is because this has happened, and not because of the operation of a dialectic of nature, that sorrow has its promise. On Christmas night something decisive happened in these depths, so that they are now full of blessing and promises and the echo of the angelic choirs is heard.

We thus have to recast all our own ideas about light. Or rather, we can now do so because we experience miracle after miracle.

And when Holy Scripture tells us that there is a "new song" in the world now that God's salvation is proclaimed—and no longer the old song of love and death—we may also speak of a new shining of earth in all its pits of darkness. This is not the old splendor with its illusory comfort and secret shadows. It is not the deceptive rhythm of joy and sorrow, day and night, winter and spring, the alternations of which seem to bring us brief redemption. No, this is the new splendor of the fact that we have been loved and visited and dearly bought by a love which caused the Child to be born in our misery and to suffer our terrible death on the cross.

What can separate us from the love of God?

Christ is here!

8

The Final Dereliction (Good Friday)

And about the ninth hour Jesus cried out with a loud voice, saying, "Eli, Eli, lema sabachthani?" that is, "My God, my God, why have you forsaken me?"

Matthew 27:46

IN THE TRACTS OF HISTORY known to us many martyrs have died—radiant figures like Stephen under the hail of stones, singing praises like the "last on the scaffold" in the story of Gertrud de le Fort, in scornfully superior resignation like Socrates.

This is now past history, but it still casts the light of its great example and arouses the veneration of later generations.

On the place of a skull, on Golgotha, however, the scene is very different. The earth quakes—and it is our earth which begins to tremble. The sun stops shining—and it is our sun which veils its face and can no longer look at this awful spectacle.

Moreover, those who come and go on the scene are men of our world.

There is the centurion under the cross. He does not know the background of the affair. But he is a religious man, and he has to confess with trembling: "This man we have executed was surely a good man." There are the women, who are affected by the terrible nature of this end, whose emotions are stirred. What overwhelms them is the human side. There are the dicers, who wile away an hour with trivialities only a few yards from the spot where their own and all human destiny is sealed. There are the sadists, the seekers of sensation, the indifferent. There is the official and cultured world with its supposed higher standpoint which tries to bring under ordinary criminal procedure that wherein God gives to history its true and proper theme. There are the "existentially" concerned disciples, agitated and helpless. And finally there are the mere spectators who have perhaps a little religious interest but who are really seeking a nervous thrill, and who care nothing whether it is provided by liturgical ceremonies in the temple or by the bloody spectacle on the hill of Golgotha.

Is not this participating world all our own world, moved or curious, gripped or indifferent? For what has brought us here today, and what is impelling others to listen to this awful story of execution either by their radio sets or as they journey though the radiant countryside of spring? The one directs his thoughts to him who here died for him as Savior, inclining to him with the prayer: "I will stand here at your side; despise me not." Another is gripped by the human splendor and loneliness of this One whom we should all remember in his dying hour, being moved by respect for his human greatness. Yet another has had much to bear in life and feels impelled to this One as a companion in his supreme grief: "Wounds must be healed by wounds." Nor are we without the dicers at the foot of the cross.

For many are comfortably eating their breakfasts or searching for jazz on the radio at this very hour when the most dreadful death of all grasps after us with it presence. Truly, this death is very different from that of the martyrs. For here at Golgotha nothing is really past. We are all implicated. And the One who dies is so infinitely different. He does not divest himself of the garment of the flesh with the contemptuous superiority of the Stoic, being then translated from this gross earth to the purer vaults of heaven. On the contrary, he utters a helpless, despairing cry in the most terrible isolation. We have here the terrors of inescapable destruction. Something very singular must have happened that One who always lived and breathed in contact with eternity should cry out in his last hour: "My God, my God, why have you forsaken me?" This death, therefore, is different from every other.

What is it, then, that takes place?

Beyond the bodily agony of crucifixion, which is terrible enough, this man suffers all the pain and sorrow which fills the heart of his Father. What dreadful rethinking is needed to understand that one thing that God suffers on our account.

There are those today who have the idea of reading the Bible as they would other great works of literature—for certain cultural reasons. They perhaps do so with the secret notion that they are studying a classical document of the religious yearning of humanity, and that they will see how far men have got in their search for the ultimate reality. But interested readers of this kind are suddenly brought to the astonishing conclusion that the theme of the Bible reverses the whole procedure, compelling them to ask rather what God has done to find man and to help him.

But once they have grasped this, to their amazement they are forced to take account of a fact which the modern man of culture might call the tragedy of God. They see that God is everywhere knocking, that he comes in blessing, judgement and visitation, that in dreadful catastrophes and the gift of rich fulfillments he wills and seeks only that men should find him and be at peace. But they also see that men do not perceive God's invitation and pursuit. He has come to you in bomb shelters and the distress of concentration camps. He has allowed you to live, and blessed you with fellow men and met you at decisive moments. But have you not always missed the great and little signs in the rush of daily life? Have you not forgotten the summons of eternity in the clamor of the passing day? We may well understand the divine lament: "Even the stork in the heavens knows her times, and the turtledove, swallow, and crane keep the time of their coming, but my people know not the rules of the LORD" (Jeremiah 8:7).

This is just what I meant when I spoke of the grief or the tragedy of God on our account. All of us have experienced the fact that our grief for someone whom we cannot help because he will not let us help him is all the greater the more we love him. You grasp how great is God's sorrow for you only when you realize how much you are loved and to what extent God is thinking about you.

And it is as if this divine grief on account of us men is concentrated in Jesus Christ—and not merely in his death. For Jesus of Nazareth experiences the divine destiny from the very first. Even when he was born his mother was refused admittance, and a manger was good enough for him. Even as an infant he had to flee. His whole life had only the one assurance, fulfilled in word and act and suffering, that God is ready to help us. His life was devoted to the one summons that we should arise and claim the joy and fulfillment which God has prepared for us.

And we are continually told that men did not understand him, they they did not want him, that they wished to go on as before, that they regarded him as a disturber of the peace when his whole aim was to restore peace. The final expression of this life is the lament: "O Jerusalem, Jerusalem.... How often would I have gathered your children together as a hen gathers her brood under her wings, and you would not!" (Matthew 23:37).

And now it is all over. The cross has been set up. This is the end. God is broken on us men. Golgotha means pain in God.

I have said that the suffering of God is so great because he loves us so much. Anyone who sees a dear friend going to the dogs, and is unable to help as he rushes step by step to destruction, knows that this is like death for himself too. For loving means complete sharing, and the misfortune of the other means pain for oneself.

This is the meaning of Good Friday for the Son of God. He bears the guilt of the world. Perhaps this sounds very dogmatic. But we can understand it clearly enough, as men, if we only see that the heart of the Savior beats with burning love for his lost and unhappy children. Because he loves them so, he understands them. And because he understands them, he suffers with them.

Perhaps there is a mother here whose son is a prisoner in Russia. Everyday she experiences afresh in her heart the lostness, the homesickness and the comfortless slave routine of her child. Indeed, this fellow–suffering of the mother's heart is perhaps more painful and tormenting than that suffered by the distant son. This is just a feeble reflection of what the Savior goes through on the hill of Golgotha. His infinite understanding leads him to suffer vicariously all that separates men from his Father. The dicers, the harlots, the executioners, the tax gatherers, the Pharisees—they do not know how lost and far from home they are. They forget it in play or gambling or dreaming. But the Son of God knows the desperate need of all of them. His love gives him such sharp vision. He knows, and he bears it all with them and for them.

Who of us really bears his own guilt? Who of us has really tried to examine himself and realistically to see and accept what is wrong in his life, his greed and anxiety and inhumanity? My God, we should go to pieces if we did. We therefore forget it all in play or dreams. We suppress it with the highly developed technique which even the most primitive can use.

But the Son of God sees all this. He sees you and me in the all–penetrating and all–revealing light of eternity. He sees in us what you and I do not see. In a single glance he takes in all the guilt which was ever incurred and all the lostness in which man was ever entangled.

Nor does he see it all in an omniscient diagnosis of the sickness of others which does not basically affect himself. He sees it like a doctor seeing on an X–ray plate the fatal disease of his own dear son. It all weighs like an intolerable burden on his own heart. We ourselves hardly feel it. But he bears it in our place as One who loves us and who therefore understands us better than we do ourselves. "He took our illnesses and bore our diseases" (Matthew 8:17). Do we now see what this means and what took place on Golgotha?

It is only thus that the Man of Sorrows can forgive us. He who really forgives must go right into the dispute. I can forgive my neighbor only when I put myself in his place, when I accept the cost of the wrong he has done me, when I experience it as though I have done it myself. The saying: "To understand all is to forgive all" is sheer nonsense.

The very opposite is the truth. It is when I forgive my neighbor that I learn to understand him—and to do so to such a degree that I suddenly stand in his place and realize that I might have acted as he did, that the same possibility lies lurking in my own heart.

What sorrow, what condescension, is thus included in the fact that the Son of God enters into our controversy with God and accepts our abandonment! For this reason we may believe in him, in him alone, that he has remitted our guilt and that he can make something new of us. We always trust those who share our difficulties. We go to pastors who we know have been taught by their own experience and suffering to plumb the depths with us. And we avoid those who may be psychologically trained and clever and efficient but who have no personal acquaintance with the things which trouble us. In war the chaplain's message is accepted only when he is ready to go to the very front lines and does not merely offer cheap comfort from the rear. Jesus fights on the very front lines at Calvary. Nothing human is alien to him. He places, or better, implicates himself so fully in our lostness that he must call out and cry in our place: "My God, my God, why have you forsaken me?"

In this saying he is altogether our Brother. In his physical agony—under terrible sufferings and thirst moving in the sunshine to a graceless end—he bears to his Father all the afflictions of hospitals, battlefields, and deathbeds. And with the afflictions he bears also the most severe and constricting anxiety which we undergo when we can no longer see the hand of the Father in what befalls us. For it is true, is it not, that we can put up with even the worst things so long as we can accept them in the sense of seeing meaning in them, of detecting, even if only from afar, the higher thoughts of God concerning them. But when we can see no meaning, no fatherly hand, the darkness closes over us. Jesus would not be our Brother if he had not suffered this too, if he had not gone down to the very lowest depths of affliction and torment where he had to cry: "My God, my God, why have you forsaken me?"—as though to say: "I could bear everything, all the loneliness, all the agony, all the heartache, if only I could snatch one glance from you and feel the impress of your little finger. But I no longer see your eyes and your hand is withdrawn from me." To suffer thus is hell.

Manfred Hausmann has depicted this vicarious agony of the Son of God in his discussion of the Sigmaringen picture of Christ under the title *One Must Watch*. The disciple John is sleeping on the breast of Christ. And while he sleeps, peaceful and relaxed, Christ looks out on the world with the glance of omniscience, and his look embraces all the sorrow of the world. He sees the filth and shame in the most secret recesses of our lives. He hears the cries of the tortured and of those racked by anxiety. He sees the sufferings of the animal creation. He sees the very smallest woe concealed from human eyes in an idyllic valley bathed in sunshine. One must watch and see all this while we sleep or go our ways dreaming and unconcerned. One must watch and take it all to heart. On Golgotha it is all concentrated into one mountainous burden resting on this single heart. Nor is this heart a stone. It is a tender heart. It loves. Nor does the burden merely rest on it. It penetrates and fills and rends it. "He took our illnesses and bore our diseases." "My God, my God, why have you forsaken me?" Do we not sense what it means that One here took our place, that he occupied the exact spot where we should have stood?

Yet in and with all this solidarity he stands out in majestic dissimilarity from us all. Like an Alpine peak, he soars up into the clouds which veil his secret and keep us to the plains. For how different is the saying: "My God, my God, why have you forsaken me?" on his lips. How it differs from our despairing cries: "Where is God?" or "How can God allow this?" or "It is all fate or illusion or chance."

We men address ourselves to the world, for we need witnesses of our despair. But he speaks to his Father. He does not say to the people who stand gaping around the cross: "My Father has forsaken me. I declare myself bankrupt. There is no Father of mine in heaven. I was leading you dreadfully astray." No, He says: "*My* God, my God, why have *you* forsaken me?" He thus grasps after the One who seems to have forsaken him. He speaks to the One who apparently does not hear. He counts on the One who seems not to exist.

Who of us, when God has apparently disappeared and we can see no more sense in things will cry to him and accuse him of forsaking us? Paradoxical though it is, this is just what Jesus did here. And for this reason he did not fall out of the concealed hands of God into an abyss; he fell into these hands. And therefore, with the underlying logic corresponding to the mysteries of God, he could finally say: "Father, into your hands I commit my spirit!" (Luke 23:46). The hands of God were there again. They were there at the right moment. And in retrospect we have to ask whether they were ever really withdrawn. Did they not always embrace him? Did they not always rest upon him in blessing?

The trouble is that we speak far too much about God in the third person. We discuss the religious question, the problem of God, the meaning of life and issues of philosophy. Or at any rate we do so if we are truly alive and are not content superficially to live for the day. In all these discussions and deliberations, however, God is only the theme. He is not a Thou with whom we speak. Hence we are miserably off the mark with our mere religious interest or philosophical concern. Hence we never find peace. The first time God is spoken of in the third person in Holy Scripture is in the story of the fall. "Did God actually say?" (Genesis 3:1). And it was the serpent who spoke like this. If we only speak of God in the third person, if we only discuss the religious question, we speak out of a deep abyss, out of the far distance. As we have said, the first discussion about God was opened by the devil. This should make us think.

On the cross, however, the One who is in the lowest depths, who has sunk to the very floor of hell, speaks with his Father in the second person: "My God, my God," and he is immediately lifted up and taken to the bosom of the Father. This should make us think.

The Thou to which he attains is his great triumph. It is because of it that the Crucified on Romanist images bears the royal crown and the insignia of majesty. For he is exalted to God because in the depths of dereliction he said: "*My* God." He claimed God as his own. And when anyone does this, the Father does not deny him. It is for this reason that the light of Easter breaks on Golgotha.

Thus the message which we now have to proclaim from Calvary's hill is that there hangs here One on whom our burden rests and on whom we may lay it—our care, our anxious fear of the future, our guilt, our broken homes, the many bankruptcies we experience in life. Here hangs One who bears all that we find intolerable and who knows all that we dare not know. And here also hangs One who for us has burst open, or rather prayed open, the way to the heart of the Father. And if I am at my wits' end when the hostile power of conscience attacks and accuses me, if I am oppressed by sickness and misfortune, if I am forsaken by men, if I can no longer see the divine hand or higher thoughts, then I may confidently repeat what the dying Savior dared to cry in his last agony: "My God, my God, why have you forsaken me?" And as I say this, the everlasting hands are there into which I may entrust myself and from which I can receive all things; and the comforting angels will come and lead me. For the way is open; One has gone before. Hence the night of Good Friday is full of the joy of Easter which is possible only in this night and at this place of the skull:

> *I cling and cling forever*
> *A member of this Head,*
> *We go our way together*
> *Wherever Christ may tread.*
> *Through death he onward goes,*
> *The world and sin and woes;*
> *He makes his way through hell*
> *And I will follow still.*

But before I may sing and praise thus, I must first come to Golgotha and say to the Man of Sorrows, the Man of my sorrows: "I will stand here at your side; despise me not."

9

Time and Eternity (Easter)

When the Sabbath was past, Mary Magdalene and Mary the mother of James and Salome bought spices, so that they might go and anoint him. And very early on the first day of the week, when the sun had risen, they went to the tomb. And they were saying to one another, "Who will roll away the stone for us from the entrance of the tomb?" And looking up, they saw that the stone had been rolled back—it was very large. And entering the tomb, they saw a young man sitting on the right side, dressed in a white robe, and they were alarmed. And he said to them, "Do not be alarmed. You seek Jesus of Nazareth, who was crucified. He has risen; he is not here. See the place where they laid him. But go, tell his disciples and Peter that he is going before you to Galilee. There you will see him, just as he told you." And they went out and fled from the tomb, for trembling and astonishment had seized them, and they said nothing to anyone, for they were afraid.

Mark 16:1–8

It is undoubtedly one of the most strange and puzzling phenomena that today countless men, old and young, members of hostile races, are gathering to listen to the reading of an ancient chronicle which tells us that some two thousand years ago Jesus of a place called Nazareth rose from the dead.

The surprising feature is that men who daily swallow the headlines of their newspapers and who are hourly instructed over the air on the development of a more than exciting modern situation should still have the time and strength to listen at all to the Easter story. Nor is it merely that they have the "time" and "strength" for this; they claim to attain to "eternity" through this story and to receive from it the strength to endure life and to be confident even in affliction and death.

Indeed, the most surprising feature of all is that they maintain that the Easter story is not ancient history but that it invades all our lives with decisive consequences. They thus say with Paul that if Christ were not risen they would be the sorriest of men, deluded deceivers, since this one great life, which was for so many the "only comfort in life and in death," would itself have been finally liquidated by death. The word of the cross: "My God, my God, why have you forsaken me?" would have been the last cry of a bankrupt ringing through an empty heaven, the night of Golgotha would have closed over it, and generation after generation would have had to grope in the hopeless shadow of this night. The one great experiment in which One entered the lists against death and the devil, against suffering and fate, on behalf of his brethren, would have failed. And only with the quiet sorrow of Good Friday could we remember this venture of a Man whom many of the most wretched and deceived described as their Savior.

Truly this story seems to have more than the status of an

ancient story. It is a decisive word concerning the lives of all of us.

For the opposite seems to be true also.

If in the one case of Jesus Christ a breach has been made in the impregnable wall of death, this story is no longer a museum piece. At a single stroke it has altered my own life. For in such circumstances Jesus Christ is a living Lord with whom I may be linked at any moment, who now speaks to me and to whom I may speak in prayer. In such circumstances we do not serve God merely at times of inner recollection when we think of him; he is in the midst of us and sees each one of us. In such circumstances the ruins and debris of our cities are no longer heaps of earth on the gigantic burying mound of the past; above these ruins there strides today the One to whom all power is given in heaven and on earth. The storms of destruction which rage on the earth proceed from the breath of his mouth. But also at work is his powerful arm which can still the elements in a moment and which with brotherly faithfulness can find and keep and comfort his own in the witches' cauldron of all terrors.

In such circumstances all this is true. We really and truly have a living Lord and we may count on him in every situation.

We thus see that the ancient record comes home to us with powerful directness. It acquires for us a breathtaking actuality. It is as it were a document on which is written my sentence of death or my title to blessedness. So urgent is this story that the one page carries with it my life's destiny. It is literally a matter of life or death.

Where can we go in this passing world, in this world which may cease to exist for us this very night, in this world of blood and tears? Where else can we go but to the open grave in the vicinity of Calvary? Shall we go to nature, which is now beginning to celebrate again the Easter resurrection of a new spring and to which the daily press points us at Easter as our only consolation? We all know how it uplifts us and gives us joy to see the buds and blossoms and to feel the breath of reawakening life. Nevertheless, nature cannot free us from the deepest puzzles of our existence. It merely plunges us into them in the greater isolation. For even in a sea of blossoms, do we not suddenly sense the autumn which will destroy it all? Even when we see a fine young man, do we not sometimes think: "You boast of the splendor of milk and purple, but the roses all wilt and fall." Even when we consider the peace of innocent nature, are we not doubly afflicted by our awareness of the violence of man and the hopeless sorrow of the world? I never felt this more than last year when I was swimming in the Bodensee and the loudspeaker announced the official news of the destruction of Hamburg.

Where else can we go but to the open grave in the vicinity of Calvary?

But how do we achieve the Easter faith? How can we bring it about that the releasing Word is spoken over our lives and the heavy stone rolled away from us?

The accounts of the resurrection are a model of the indirect and discreet way in which the Bible indicates an event which cannot really be described in words. For obviously one cannot speak of the resurrection as one would describe a business set back or an ordinary historical event. What takes place around this tomb is all bathed in an indirect and puzzling light. We are not really told about the resurrection as such. No sensationalism or curiosity tries to tear aside the veil of mystery. We see only the reactions and effects of this tremendous event on the disciples and the women.

It is no accident that the women are the first at the grave of the Savior. The men are sunk in consuming disappointment and bitterness and have gone into hiding like wounded animals. We know their trouble. Their Christian view of things has been completely shattered. They are, as it were, rudely awakened at Calvary. How could they have thought that this One was different from all of us? How could they have thought that he alone was exempt from guilt and death and mortality? To be sure, there is nothing shameful or derogatory in dying. We all have to die. There is even a certain glory in dying for an idea, as Socrates did. But when this One dies, even for his ideas, it is a catastrophe. For he is not a man who has just brought a new teaching, that God is love, that there are higher thoughts concerning our lives and that the kingdom of God will come to us. If the Nazarene had simply brought new teaching such as this, his death would have been sad but it would not have been a catastrophe. For his teaching might well have survived him, as in the case of Socrates or Plato.

But Jesus is not on the same plane as Socrates or Plato. He has not merely brought teaching on the way in which God and man can again attain to peace and fellowship. He has advanced the claim that he can authoritatively close the gap between God and man, that he can restore the world deranged by pain, unrighteousness and enmity against God, that he is more than a match for the awful majesty of death.

If this is so, however, it is a true catastrophe if he himself is overwhelmed by death, if the wicked hands of men can throw this divine life, this supposedly divine life, into the tomb.

It is because this seems to be so that the men skulk in corners and only the women come to the grave. They want to offer their sorrowful remembrances to the dead. They come in the same mood as brings people to church on Good Friday. This noble man was broken, but we cannot forget that for a time he brought light and comfort into our lives and gave us in unsuspecting childhood the dream of a Father in heaven and of a loving Savior.

None of the women really believes that he has risen. Their only thought is: "Who will roll away the stone for us?" They are seeking the dead among the dead. And when they learn that he is risen, they are psychologically so little prepared for the event, and it is so terrifying and shattering, that they are overcome by fear and trembling, and they take to panic–stricken flight and do not tell anybody.

We do not know what really happened or how it happened. The event lies in a zone of silence. It is invested with a veil of mystery. We know only what precedes and what follows. What precedes is that the disciples are sunk in hopelessness and depression. What follows is that new faith takes possession of them. We see how in a moment of absolute and objective hopelessness, in the hell of the most terrible doubts, there suddenly arises the Church against which the gates of hell cannot prevail, which encloses us today two thousand years later, and which will one day unite the generation of the Last Day.

There may be some who understand this. I myself do not. Nevertheless, it happened; and it still happens today.

But the question arises how we today can be sure that we have a living Savior. It is one thing to have been there and quite another merely to be told about it. Lessing saw this, and his words betray the resignation of a later generation separated from the resurrection by almost two thousand years and by the uncertainty of historical records.

We may thus rephrase the question and ask how *we* may attain to Easter certainty. it is surely obvious that this certainty which is stronger than death and which can give us our only comfort in life and in death cannot possibly be given by historical records, even though they may be quite authentic, as the Easter stories undoubtedly are. For all those of us who think to find, and have actually found, this comfort in Jesus Christ, it is quite intolerable that our faith should be dependent on the existing state or fashion of historical scholarship.

The Easter story, however, teaches us that this is not so. It is relevant to note how Jesus Christ himself handles the question of the resurrection in the parable of Dives and Lazarus. The rich man sits in hell and thinks of his frivolous brothers who are still alive and who might well stand under the threat of a similar fate. He considers how they can be given a salutary shock to jostle them off the way of destruction. He conceives the idea of asking Abraham to send a message to tell them about the torments of hell. But Abraham shows him that they have Moses and the prophets. In other words, they have the Word of God, and this should be enough. If they do not believe this Word, they would not believe even though one rose from the dead.

We can say just the same of the disciples on Easter morning. They could never have believed that the dead Jesus had risen from the dead if they had not believed his Word. Other explanations could then have been given, for example, that his body had been stolen or taken away. A miracle has never yet brought anyone to faith, since it is always open to other interpretations. The empty tomb did not bring the disciples to faith. Something very different happened. Before the empty tomb, and under the impression of the words of the angel, scales fell from their eyes. In the Easter light of the third day they suddenly saw that all the words and acts of Jesus pointed to the fact that death could not hold him. It was of these words and acts that they had now to think.

If someone could say: "Your sins are forgiven you," and the person concerned really arose and went away a new man, this One could only be somebody who was not implicated in the destiny of this world which has dashed itself on God and broken away from him. If someone could say: "Young man, I say to you, arise," and the dead really arose and was restored to his sorrowing mother, this One could only be somebody who was stronger than death. If someone could say: "In me you shall find rest for your souls," and men really walked in fellowship with him, this One could only be somebody who himself lived in a peace and fellowship with God which could not be broken or severed by anything, not even by death. The saying: "Come to me, all who labor and are heavy laden," could be said only by somebody who himself understood weariness and sorrow, who shared it as a Brother, but whose life was nourished from other sources and from whose body flowed streams of living and inexhaustible water.

All this is what the disciples suddenly and unexpectedly saw in the light of Easter. The whole life of the Savior as he went through the land, healing and helping, forgiving and giving new beginnings, was opened up to them. It was as if the key to his innermost secrets was unexpectedly pressed into their hands. They suddenly saw that when he went about the earth and they shared his daily life, they had not really known him. To be sure, their hearts had burned, and they had had the sense of a gigantic figure towering over them. But now they realized who had been traveling with them. Now a light shone on his puzzling sayings, and heaven opened over the One whom they had regarded as one man, albeit the greatest, among others, but who was in fact the Wholly Other who had come from the eternity of the Father and entered into their everyday life for a short period.

Hence it is not surprising that only those who had accompanied him and lived in fellowship with him were witnesses of the resurrection. Only among them could there be a profitable fusion between what they had experienced with him and the awe–inspiring new thing which happened to them on Easter morning. Only in them could there be the fusion from which there suddenly sprang the spark of faith to kindle generation after generation as the light of the living Christ and to bring the torch of God into the darkest valleys or our pilgrimage. The resurrection is a fact which is open only to faith, and it is a profound and decisive aspect of the Easter story that in spite of the empty tomb the disciples could not see the mystery directly but had to believe the word of the angels. The word! It is only because they do this, and are thus content with Moses and the prophets, that there is revealed to them the mystery that One has here risen from the dead.

The fact that it is revealed only to faith distinguishes the resurrection from the return of the Lord on the Last Day. The resurrection is certain only to those who are resolved to live with him, who are won by his words and his whole person, who give themselves unconditionally to him. Those who will not do this may pass him by; they may obliterate the bloody drama of Golgotha and the divine miracle of the third day; they may act as though these things had never taken place, as though there were only newspapers, the radio, war and peace, birth and death, as though this moment had never been. But one day this dream of the wordly will be over. One day the eyes which were wild with hatred will have to see him as he is. One day the fists which clenched against him will open in a gesture of worship. One day the knees which were stiff and independent will bow before him. This will be the moment when faith may see what it has believed and unbelief will have to see what it has not.

We are thus asked whether we are ready to commit ourselves, to entrust our lives, to this King over all the powers of death. For only in this way can we have the certainty of Easter. Only in this way can we overcome death and the fear of death. We need a personal relationship to him.

Many people say that Easter is a sign that life always conquers death. They thus compare it to spring, when nature celebrates its resurrection and the imperishable and triumphant force of life finds expression.

This view is shockingly mistaken. There is no resurrection in nature. We may just as truly say that everything is as the grass which blooms and quickly fades. Every spring carries within it autumn, every birth death. It is simply a matter of mood or temperament whether we emphasize the one side or the other.

Fundamentally, do we not realize this clearly today? We who have gone through so much surely know that the loved one snatched from our side will not return or rise again with a new spring. We surely see that the home which is perhaps a heap of rubble will not come back with the old atmosphere and memories even though our things are replaced ten times over.

It is just not true that life, or at any rate personal life, triumphs over death. The well–known saying of Goethe is true of many great things and men which were in our lives once but will never return: "What is past cannot return; but if it went down brightly, there is a long afterglow." Humanly speaking, this afterglow is all that is left to us.

But when we grasp with pitiless realism this fact of mortality, we may also say what the Easter story so surprisingly and at first so terrifyingly discloses, namely, that Jesus Christ has overcome death and that those who are in him, who live in fellowship with him, will not taste death.

One might reduce the Gospel to the very simple formula that at the very deepest level Jesus Christ unites the destiny of us men with his own.

This is true in both directions. First, he takes our life in all its severity upon himself. He is tempted as we are. He bears our guilt. He suffers our isolation and on the cross goes through all the stages of dereliction in our place.

But the converse is also true. He takes us up into his life. Living by his eternal fellowship with the Father, he makes me his brother and draws me into his own fellowship with the Father. Living in powerful triumph over death, he makes me his brother and companion and takes me through the dark night of death to Paradise. "Is the Head alone to go, And leave the member here below?" or, "And I will follow still,"—that is what we sing in our Easter hymns.

Perhaps I am afraid of death. I shudder at the thought of this final, irrevocable parting. The dreadful night of death fills me with anxious thoughts. But now there is One to go with me when my time comes, and he is waiting on the other side.

Perhaps I dread what might happen. I am afraid of the unborn terrors which old Europe might yet bring forth, or of what might threaten in the East. Perhaps I am full of fear when I get the reek of fire and catastrophe in the ruins of our cities. But here is rest. The oceans of this uncertain world are no more than a puddle in the hand of my Savior, as Gorch Fock has put it. The continents and mountains are only an ear of corn in his finger. And this hand is the hand of the Victor. One day, when all human hands have fallen and perished, it will be stretched over the earth as the final hand. In a royal gesture it will open the graves and summon the skeletons to him.

The Easter faith, then, is not just an upward glance to satisfy my curiosity about the mysterious hereafter. It is a summons of the Prince of Life to the present hour of life: "Be reconciled to God; seize the new life which is offered; bury your old man in the grave where Jesus lay. Now is the accepted time; now his arms are open to you; now the Master is seeking companions." Perhaps God will require your soul this night. Who knows? Be supremely careful, then, that your soul is in the one, good hand which can still the waves, open the graves, bind up wounds and cancel guilt. Then the dark companion cannot cross the circle which the Savior has drawn around you. Then your coffin will be a couch on which you will awaken when the morning of resurrection dawns. Then the burial place, whether at home, on the high seas or in a distant land, will be a plot where you will sleep as a seed in the eternal sowing of God, to ripen on the day of harvest. Then you may make the royal Easter confession of one who is great in the kingdom of God:

"Therefore, when I die—though now I die no more— and someone finds my skull, may this skull preach to him as follows:

I have no eyes, yet I see him;

I have no brain nor understanding, yet I know him;

I have no lips, yet I kiss him,

I have no tongue, yet I praise him with all you who call upon his name;

I am a hard skull, yet I am softened and melted in his love; I lie without in the churchyard, yet I am within Paradise.

All suffering is forgotten because of his great love when for us he bore His cross and went to Calvary."

10

The Light of Pentecost (Whitsunday)

THE SO−CALLED MAN in the street—a very dubious construct of thought—usually regards Pentecost as the most strange and baffling of all the Christian festivals. He can find no key to it. Christmas, Good Friday and Easter are concrete. A child is born, a noble man dies on the gallows and a dead man is seen again, as we often see loved ones who have been taken from us, at least in imagination. But there is nothing concrete about Pentecost. The idea that in an unheard of and inconceivable event tongues of flame sat on the heads of the disciples and that there was then a counter−miracle to the confusion of tongues, all linguistic barriers being overthrown, is so fantastic that the imagination cannot grasp it. We all see at once that here is an event which could not be photographed. The image of the flame enhances the impression of inconceivability. It is obviously designed to indicate the inexpressible. It is a stammering figure, stammering out something of which we can have no more similitude or image than of God himself.

The event of Pentecost does in fact denote a mystery. It tells us that there is a sphere of reality—and to this belongs all that has to do with God—into which we cannot penetrate at our pleasure, but only as a door is opened to us. The sphere of arithmetic is one that I can enter at will if I have a modicum of intelligence. I can see at once that two and two make four. I do not even have to be taught this at school. Again, the mysteries of the weather or of natural growth in my garden are fairly accessible to my grasp, even if there is a good deal of play between what the ordinary gardener knows of the growth of plants and the orders of chromosomes investigated by the expert. Knowledge of the personal aspects of life, however, is rather more mysterious. How do I know what motherly love is? Let us take the unfortunate case of one who, like Casper Hauser, never lived in the warm glow of motherly love, and let us ask ourselves what he could say about it. He could obviously do little more than make certain observations, as, for example, that he had seen a mother selflessly tending an incurably sick child instead of abandoning it as many animals abandon their unfit young; or that he had seen a mother forgive and continue to love a rebellious child or even an older son who had gone astray. But he could not really enter into these things. They would be simply the letters of a mysterious document whose characters he could describe but which he could not understand. One cannot know motherly love in the same way as one can know a universally accessible principle of arithmetic. To know motherly love a specific condition has to be fulfilled. One must have had a mother and one must have been loved by her. One must live in a certain state in order to have this knowledge.

It is exactly the same with God. We may talk and dispute about him endlessly, just as orphans may talk about the symptoms of motherly love without ever penetrating to its true essence. But we can really speak about the Father in heaven only when we are his children. We can really speak about Jesus Christ only when we are his brothers. We can really speak about both only when we love them just as a child can really speak about the mystery of the mother only when it loves this mother.

But how can we love God? Love is always evoked, and it is evoked by being loved. How can I love my mother if I do not experience physically and emotionally her faithfulness, her constant readiness, her self–sacrifice for me?

When we realize this, we are well on the way to understanding Pentecost. For Pentecost tells us two things, the one negative and the other positive.

The negative point is that what is recorded in the Bible, for example, the story of the Savior's birth or the dreadful event of Golgotha, is all hidden and dead, it is all a mysterious document, so long as we see it only from outside and read it like a novel or a collection of short stories. For in this case it is only one group of happenings among so many others. A young mother has a child; a man sacrifices himself for a cause. Such things can move us. And the flood of sentimentality surrounding Christmas and Good Friday is a sign that we are stirred and even gripped by them. But it does not mean that we understand. And so long as we do not, our nerves are affected rather than our hearts.

The positive side is that we can attain to a true understanding of these stories only if we note that here the miracle of divine love comes upon me, that here my Savior is born, that here he dies for me. I cannot see of myself this personal application to my own heart. We are in quite a different sphere from that of the principle that two and two make four. I have to be drawn into this event by higher hands. A light has to be kindled for me. Luther speaks of this when he refers to the enlightening power of the Holy Spirit. Basically this is something very simple. It is not at all a question of ecstasy, enthusiasm or fanaticism. One has only to ask an experienced Christian what is the place of the Holy Spirit in his life. He will usually give the cool and sober answer: "I was given religious instruction like you. I did well, and perhaps even very well, in this branch of study. I knew all the main stories in both Testaments, and my younger brothers and sisters were enthralled when I told the stories to them." He might then go on to say: "I later studied theology and found out how the stories arose and what scholars have to say about them. But suddenly—I do not know how—it came home to me that they were all written for me. This happened when I began to take them seriously and tried to live as they prescribed, 'as though' they were the Word of God. Once I did this, and obeyed them, they suddenly began to light up from within. A miracle now happened to me, and for the first time I noticed that what I had previously known was only the curves and strokes and dots of a mysterious document which in spite of all my knowledge I did not understand."

This is roughly how the experienced Christian will answer us. And in so doing he is describing exactly what is meant by the Pentecostal miracle of enlightenment. The Whitsun address of Peter deals only with things which he had always known; he recounts the Old Testament history of the divine salvation. But now this is lighted up from within, just as invisible writing on glass is suddenly legible when a light shines behind the glass. The data were the same, but they were now so completely different that men were overpowered by them.

I will close with a comparison which will perhaps make plain what I have been saying. A cathedral has beautiful stained-glass windows. If I walk around outside, I see only a dull gray–black which tells me nothing. I am telling the literal truth if I go home and say that I have seen these windows. Yet I have not really seen them because I have seen them only from outside and therefore on the wrong side. Only when I enter into the sanctuary do they begin to glow and to overwhelm me with the power of their colors. Then the gray is changed into the glory of the divine stories illustrated by one who was himself enlightened.

The message of Pentecost teaches us that we must approach the sacred words from the right place if we are to see their radiance and to realize that they are addressed to us. We must be already in the cathedral if we are to see this. And the message of Pentecost gives us the promise that, if we will let ourselves be drawn in, we too may enter.

Reviews of *Between God and Satan:*

"In this urgent book we see sharply contrasted blacks and whites, Satan and God, and, in between, man, continuously confronted with decisive choice between the two. It is a moving book, with many insights into our Lord's bitter struggle and many insights, too, into our own temptations...."

C. L. Mitton

"... a penetrating commentary on human existence.... For those who are willing to linger with it, there is a rich experience in store. And for the preacher, there is enough here for a dozen sermons!"

Howard Hageman

"It deserves to be read by many pastors, teachers, laymen, to refresh not only preaching and teaching but faith itself."

Concordia Theological Monthly

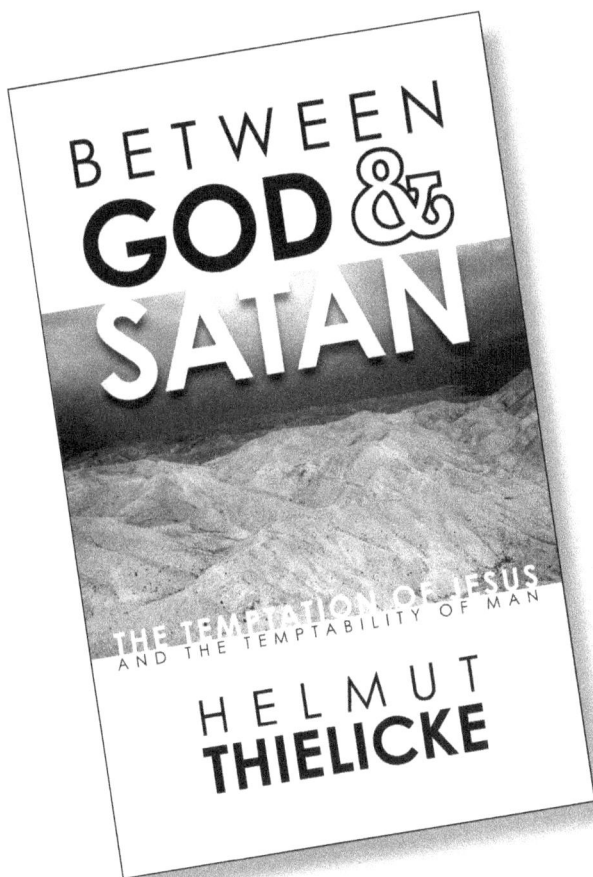

"Jesus Christ came to us to suffer temptation, to suffer our fate with regard to God, and to become our brother. Let us go to him in the desert to see what he had to endure, and how he had to fight, so as thus to become our brother. Here we shall learn who we are and how it stands with this our world....

The desert is our world; the tempter is our tempter; the forty days and forty nights are our time, and we are Jesus, for here he stands in our stead.

Who are we then, O God, who are we?"

From Chapter 1 of *Between God and Satan*

9780984491704